ABRAHAM LINCOLN

AN ILLUSTRATED LIFE AND LEGACY

THOMAS F. SCHWARTZ
AND THOMAS CUSSANS

THUNDER BAY
P·R·E·S·S

San Diego, California

Thunder Bay Press
An imprint of the Baker & Taylor Publishing Group
10350 Barnes Canyon Road, San Diego, CA 92121
www.thunderbaybooks.com

Text and Design Copyright © Carlton Books Limited 2013

All notations of errors or omissions should be addressed to Thunder Bay Press, Editorial Department, at the
above address. All other correspondence (author inquiries, permissions) concerning the content of this book
should be addressed to Carlton Books Limited, 20 Mortimer Street, London W1T 3JW, United Kingdom.

ISBN-13: 978-1-60710-936-5
ISBN-10: 1-60710-936-0

Printed in China

1 2 3 4 5 17 16 15 14 13

Contents

Introduction

Abraham Lincoln never looked upon his youth with great fondness. He rarely discussed his early life, claiming that his childhood in Kentucky and Indiana represented nothing more than the "short and simple annals of the poor." Thomas Lincoln, Abraham Lincoln's father, was a subsistence farmer who supplemented the family income as a carpenter, a skill passed on to his son. The hardscrabble of the frontier was made more palatable when the young autodidact Abraham learned to read. Largely self-taught, education provided opportunities that freed individuals from the intensive manual labor required by farming.

Rumors of the rich Illinois soil lured Thomas Lincoln to relocate his family from Indiana to the neighboring state in 1830. The following year, aged 22, Abraham Lincoln left his family to set out on his own. Career opportunities called him to the village of New Salem. During his six-year stay, Lincoln explored several careers that included store clerk, store owner, postmaster, surveyor, state legislator, and lawyer. The practice of law and politics remained Lincoln's twin ambitions throughout life. Despite its briefly booming economy, New Salem proved a failure for Lincoln and, selling his stake in a local store, he moved to Springfield, Illinois, on April 15, 1837, to begin afresh in Illinois's new state capitol. It was here that he met Mary Todd, a vivacious socialite from Lexington, Kentucky. They were married after a stormy courtship, raised a family, and settled down in a middle-class home. Mary always promoted her husband's political ambitions whether as a United States representative in Congress, the two times he battled for the United States Senate, or in his presidential race for the White House.

The fragile American experiment in self-government fractured in the decade of the 1850s. A nation that claimed the equality of men also embraced the enslavement of blacks. In claiming that slaves were property, not citizens with rights, the Constitution and Roger Taney's Supreme Court were at odds with a growing anti-slavery sentiment sweeping the Northern states. A federal law was passed guaranteeing the return of fugitive slaves to their Southern masters, but this provoked even greater outrage by anti-slavery forces. In spite of Lincoln's assurances to protect slavery in states where it existed but prevent its expansion in territories where it did not, Southerners remained skeptical. Lincoln's lopsided sectional victory in his campaign for the presidency—he received no support in the South—revived Southern fears that not only slavery, but its leadership positions in Congress and the federal courts, would be threatened.

The firing upon Fort Sumter on April 12, 1861, began the bloodiest conflict in the history of the United States. It was a war that neither side was prepared to fight. The systematic concerns of mobilization, command and control structures, financing, and the possibility of foreign interference were only part of Lincoln's problems. The war directly confronted the issues of slavery and emancipation. If slavery was to be ended, what form would emancipation take? If slaves were legally viewed as property, they might be confiscated for military use in time of war for military purposes, but what of their status in peacetime? And what of the status of slaves in the border states that remained loyal to the Union and were not in rebellion against the federal government?

Lincoln's handling of the war and his explanation to the American public of why the war was worth fighting and why emancipation was necessary inspired his generation, and continue to inspire us today. Claiming in his Gettysburg Address that America was "dedicated to the proposition that all men are created equal," Abraham Lincoln also hoped the war would foment "a new birth of freedom," introducing some four million former slaves to the fruits of a free society. In spite of political opposition, Lincoln successfully advanced a constitutional amendment that forever ended slavery.

The cost of the war in blood and treasure was staggering. At least 620,000 individuals died. In the North, this meant that 16 out of every 100 men of military age perished. In the South, one out of every five soldiers was killed or died from disease. Capital costs were equally dramatic. It is estimated the North spent over six billion dollars on the war while secession cost the South between five and eight billion. John Wilkes Booth was so angered by the devastation of the South as well as by Lincoln's efforts to extend voting privileges to freed blacks that he assassinated the president. Lincoln never lived to see his greatest legacy: that, as he said in his Gettysburg Address, the "government of the people, by the people, for the people, shall not perish from the earth."

Lincoln's Ancestors

1600–1800

In 1860 American presidential candidate Abraham Lincoln was asked to send some facts about his life to newspaper editor Jesse W. Fell of the Bloomington, Illinois, *Pantagraph*, for an article published on February 11 of that year. "There is not much of it," Lincoln apologized, "for the reason, I suppose, that there is not much of me."

Lincoln's modesty reveals important elements of his character. He knew little of his family history, claiming that his parents were from "undistinguished families." And what he knew was not a family history of success and leisure but of trials and hard work. Indeed, Abraham Lincoln's many achievements resulted from his own efforts of study and persistence to reach his goals. He lived at a time when "self-made" men and women were presented as examples of how people could better themselves, both materially and, more importantly, morally, by improving their characters.

Lincoln did know that he was named after his grandfather, Abraham, who was killed by Native Americans in Kentucky, leaving a widow, three sons, and two daughters alone to fend for themselves. When he was in Congress, several letters with other correspondents who shared his surname allowed Lincoln to trace his family back two generations to Virginia and Pennsylvania, but no further. Despite his intellectual curiosity, Lincoln remained in the dark about his family genealogy.

Today, we know that his ancestors came from Hingham in eastern England, in the weaving area of the county of Norfolk. The family improved

in status, perhaps reaching its height with Richard Lincoln of Hingham and Swanton Morley. Whatever fortune he made, however, quickly disappeared in an unfortunate fourth marriage. Edward Lincoln, Richard's eldest son, returned to Hingham, where a son, Samuel, was born in 1622. This child became the great-great-great-great-grandfather of the sixteenth U.S. president. Because Hingham was located in the heart of the fabric industry, Samuel Lincoln was naturally drawn to that profession. Cheaper fabric from Europe,

ABOVE The Congregationalist Church at Hingham, Massachusetts, which was built in 1680, shortly after Lincoln's family lived there.

LEFT The house built in the early eighteenth century by Lincoln's great-great-great-grandfather, Mordecai Lincoln, for his second wife.

OPPOSITE ABOVE The house where Lincoln's father, Thomas Lincoln, was born, on Linville Creek, Rockingham County, Virginia.

OPPOSITE BELOW A color engraving of an Indian attack on a settlement, similar to those that would have taken place on the Kentucky frontier.

as well as persecution of religious dissenters known as Puritans, led to a mass emigration from this region of England to towns in the New World colony of Massachusetts. Apprenticed as a weaver to Francis Lawes, Samuel Lincoln duly emigrated from Hingham, England, to Salem, Massachusetts, in 1637. Upon completion of his apprenticeship, he went to Hingham, Massachusetts, where his two brothers had settled.

The first four generations of the Lincoln lineage became successful farmers and blacksmiths in the colonies of Massachusetts, New Jersey, Pennsylvania, and Virginia. Migration represented the norm; four out of five males moved from their place of birth. That the Lincolns were always on the move to find cheaper and more productive land mirrored what most other Americans were doing at this time: seeking a better life.

Abraham Lincoln, the grandfather of the future president, was born in Virginia, but moved his family to Kentucky to better his fortunes. Upon his death, all his wealth went to his eldest son, Mordecai, and nothing to his youngest son, Thomas. At the age of eight, Thomas Lincoln was left without an inheritance and became a "wandering laboring boy," according to his son. Through hard work in manual labor and carpentry, however, Thomas Lincoln accumulated enough money to purchase land of his own. Once financially secure, he took the next step of seeking a wife and raising a family.

CONFLICT ON THE FRONTIER

Attacks by Native Americans, or Indians, as they were known at the time, were a regular occurrence in New World settlements. From 1783 to 1790, an estimated 1,500 settlers were killed or captured in raids. The most fearsome tribe that populated Kentucky was the Shawnee. Frontier mothers warned their children to go to bed without a sound "or the Shawnees will catch you." Eventually, the increasing number of European settlers and a growing military presence removed the threat from Kentucky, allowing permanent settlements to flourish.

Lincoln's Childhood

1809–1830

Had Thomas Lincoln begun farming with a secure title to his property, he would have been a prosperous man. During his time in Kentucky, he owned three farms totaling nearly a thousand acres—only to lose them all because of faulty titles. Surveys at the time were often improperly conducted, and changing government land policies created an environment of overlapping claims to the same property.

In 1803, Thomas Lincoln purchased what he believed to be a 238-acre farm for £118 (or approximately $500), improved the property, and felt financially secure enough to marry Nancy Hanks on June 10, 1806. The following year, a daughter, Sarah, was born. Thomas took his family to a new 300-acre farm on Nolin Creek. It was here, on February 12, 1809, that a son, Abraham, was born. The few public documents still in existence reveal that Thomas Lincoln was an upright citizen, serving on juries, petitioning for the construction of roads, and paying taxes. He supplemented his income as a carpenter, a skill he passed on to his son. Thomas also joined the Mount Separate Baptist Church—a church that opposed slavery. In 1811, there were 1,627 white settlers in Hardin County, while 1,007 slaves populated the area. Slave labor provided unfair competition for wage-earners such as Thomas Lincoln and his family.

In 1815, Thomas Lincoln paid cash for a third farm, after selling his first at a loss because of a defective title. This same problem affected his two other properties. By 1816, he decided to move his family to the newly created state of Indiana, by the Little Pigeon Creek near Gentryville, where, this time, he bought land directly from the federal government.

Indiana provided Abraham Lincoln with his most vivid childhood memories. It was here that his father taught him how to farm, wield an axe to clear the land, and make fencing and firewood. Young Abraham also received his first formal schooling in Indiana. In 1818 his mother died as a result of milk sickness. A year later, Thomas Lincoln returned to Kentucky and married a widow, Sarah (Sally) Bush Johnston, who was an old childhood friend. The new Lincoln household now held five children: Sarah and Abraham Lincoln, and Elizabeth, Matilda, and John Johnston. Dennis Hanks, who was Nancy Hanks Lincoln's cousin, also stayed in the cabin. Both Sarah and Abraham quickly warmed to their new stepmother.

ABOVE The Kentucky cabin that is claimed to have been Abraham Lincoln's birthplace.

BELOW LEFT The tombstone of Nancy Hanks Lincoln, Abraham Lincoln's mother, who died from milk sickness on October 5, 1818, when she was 34.

WHAT WAS MILK SICKNESS?

White snakeroot, a plant that thrived in shady forested areas, often attracted cattle, especially in hot summers. After ingesting white snakeroot, cows began to show signs of "trembles" and died within three days. The trembles were brought on by a substance contained in the white flowers of the snakeroot called tremetol, which is a neurotoxin. Typically, tremetol was transmitted to humans through the milk of an affected cow. Symptoms in humans ranged from dizziness, nausea, and vomiting to stomach pains, unquenchable thirst, and a rancid breath odor. Victims eventually fell into a coma and died within a week or less.

Abraham Lincoln once remarked that his "father taught him to work but never learned him to love it." His innate intellectual curiosity about the world around him made Abraham increasingly less fond of manual labor. Books helped him escape the limitation of the frontier by expanding his mental horizons.

During the late summer of 1826, Lincoln took a job operating a ferry. Two businessmen, in gratitude for being able to catch a steamboat, each tossed a silver half-dollar into Lincoln's boat. It was the most money he had ever seen, and it seemed to prove to him that an emerging market economy offered more than a life of farming. Lincoln's greatest adventure occurred two years later in 1828, when he helped a friend, Allen Gentry, pilot a flatboat of goods from Indiana down the Ohio and Mississippi Rivers to New Orleans. It exposed young Abraham to the wider world of commerce made possible by river transport.

Thomas Lincoln, hearing of more productive lands in Illinois that did not have milk sickness, soon sold his holdings in Indiana and headed west. His son, Abraham, led one of three oxen teams on the journey that ended with the family settling just outside Decatur, Illinois.

ABOVE LEFT Sarah Bush Johnston, Lincoln's stepmother.

BELOW A late nineteeth-century photograph of Lincoln's Indiana home.

Lincoln the Young Man

1830-1837

The winter of 1830–1831 produced an unusual amount of snow in Illinois, combined with prolonged cold temperatures. Hogs and cattle died in the fields, and it was often difficult to find firewood. Thomas Lincoln decided to return to Indiana once the spring thaw commenced—the same time as his son found another opportunity to take a flatboat of goods, belonging to New Salem merchant Denton Offutt, to New Orleans. In March 1831, Abraham Lincoln helped build the flatboat in Sangamon Town, Illinois, near Springfield. En route from Sangamon Town to New Salem, Illinois, the flatboat got caught on the mill dam and was freed only by the young Lincoln's ingenuity.

Upon Lincoln's return to New Salem in July 1831, Denton Offutt was so impressed by the young man's ability that he offered him a job as a clerk in his New Salem store. Offutt left the store and the New Salem property to Abraham Lincoln and Charles Maltby, the other store clerk, when he left

Illinois hounded by legal problems. Lincoln retained this property and the store, which he used as his residence throughout his stay at New Salem.

New Salem offered an opportunity for Lincoln to test his ambitions, experience many different careers, and discover the opposite sex. For a brief period in 1832, when yet another Indian conflict, the Black Hawk War, threatened settlements in northern Illinois, Lincoln volunteered with the Illinois militia. As was customary at the time, military divisions elected their officers and Lincoln was chosen as captain. After his first enlistment ended, Lincoln reenlisted as a private and served two more stints. Although he never saw any combat, he remembered the experience as one of deep satisfaction.

In 1833, Lincoln purchased several stocks of goods with a business partner, William F. Berry, and opened a store, but it failed. Fortunately, he was able to gain an appointment as postmaster from President Andrew Jackson. This job provided him with a modest income and access to newspapers that were

WHO WAS ANNE RUTLEDGE?

Daughter of New Salem tavern owner James Rutledge, Anne was engaged to John McNamar, a local New Salem merchant. When McNamar left New Salem to travel east on family business, he remained away for months on end. According to oral tradition, it was during this period that Abraham Lincoln fell in love with Anne and wanted to marry her once McNamar returned and she could break the engagement. In the summer of 1835, however, she became ill with "brain fever" and died, leaving Lincoln inconsolable.

The evidence for the romance is based upon oral tradition that was documented almost four decades after the fact. Historians remain divided on the reliability of this testimony, given the vagaries of human memory. What is well documented is Lincoln's engagement to Mary Owens, one year after Anne Rutledge's death.

OPPOSITE Abraham Lincoln's wrestling match with Jack Armstrong won him the respect of New Salem residents.

ABOVE LEFT Lincoln returning from the Black Hawk War in which he was a captain in the Illinois militia.

RIGHT A photograph of Lincoln's former fiancée Mary Owens.

BELOW An interior photograph of the reconstructed store Lincoln owned with William F. Berry.

sent through the mail. In early 1834, Lincoln was appointed deputy surveyor of Sangamon County and taught himself surveying. For the next three years, he surveyed roads, town plans, school lots, and farms. His election to the state legislature in 1834 introduced him to the finest legal minds in the state. Several individuals encouraged Lincoln to study law, which he finally opted to do in 1836.

Lincoln was always awkward around women, yet he seemed more at ease with the local tavern owner's daughter, Anne Rutledge. Unfortunately, she died in 1835, one of many victims of malaria or typhoid. Within a year, Lincoln was engaged to another woman, Mary Owens, whom he had met at New Salem; soon, however, he wanted to end the relationship. Trying to do so honorably for both sides, Lincoln indicated that Mary "would have to be poor without the means of hiding your poverty." Mary eventually broke off the engagement herself, later commenting that "Lincoln was deficient in those little links which make up the chain of [a] woman's happiness."

New Salem's population began to decrease, and by 1840 it had become a ghost town. Petersburg, a town several miles to the north, became the county seat of the newly created Menard County, and attracted many families from New Salem. Lincoln, however, saw that his future lay at the newly designated state capitol at Springfield.

On April 15, 1837, Abraham Lincoln left New Salem and arrived in Springfield. He was 28 years old and would live exactly 28 more years. The move to Springfield thus marked the midpoint in Lincoln's life.

Lincoln: A Typical American?

1809–1865

The short answer to this otherwise reasonable question is an emphatic "no." In the early days of his political career, seeking office as a more or less small-time Illinois lawyer, Lincoln consistently sought to portray himself as the tongue-tied "Honest Abe," a backwoodsman who had stumbled into elected office and who, invariably badly dressed, could then offer little more than humorously expressed home-spun virtues. He hardly seemed an opponent to take seriously.

Even after being elected president in 1860, he arrived in Washington still apparently exuding little more than this sense of clumsy, frontier good sense. Political opponents, not unreasonably supposing themselves more worldly, believed that here was a man to be readily manipulated.

"Honest Abe" left them consistently flat-footed. He was as susceptible to the lures of high office as any other ambitious man—a point he never denied. Yet under his apparent golly-gosh exterior he proved a supreme master of the

LEFT Charles Teck's 1945 statue of the young Lincoln. It shows him barefoot and with book in hand, evidence of humble beginnings and of an inherent love of learning.

OPPOSITE RIGHT Lincoln and his youngest son, Thomas, universally known as Tad, in December 1864. As a parent, Lincoln was remarkably indulgent, as he needed to be with Tad, who was not so much high-spirited as extremely badly behaved.

OPPOSITE LEFT An anti-Republican cartoon of September 1860 showing Lincoln atop a rail—in fact a fence post—supported by an improbable pairing of a black slave and Horace Greeley, outspoken editor of the *New York Tribune*.

darker political arts, confounding opponents at every turn. But infinitely more important was his response to the two moral imperatives that confronted his presidency: the primacy of the Union and the legitimacy of slavery. His defense of the first was absolute. For Lincoln, the United States represented a daringly unprecedented experiment in democracy, with human liberty its central theme. His presidential oath demanded its defense. It was not a charge he was prepared to give up.

He was very much more circumspect about the second. In order to retain the delicate loyalty of the border states, he initially consistently supported their right to own slaves. No less tellingly, he similarly asserted the war was being fought not to outlaw slavery in the Confederacy but to prevent its spread to the western territories. Not for the first time, Lincoln was forced into the murky realities of compromise.

This exceedingly delicate balancing act produced a series of violently complicated contradictions. One of his first acts as president was the suspension of habeas corpus. At a stroke, this relentless defender of human liberty overturned almost its most fundamental principle, that no one can be incarcerated without trial. That said, there was always a sense that Lincoln took a particular delight in confounding the world.

Yet Lincoln, husband, father, politician, general, seer, was not just dealing with abstract notions of political theory and the daily details of political

THE RAIL CANDIDATE

Not entirely unreasonably, Lincoln's political opponents in the 1860 presidential elections accused him of a degree of political opportunism in his attempts to reconcile the apparently incompatible goals of the new Republican Party with those of the Negro slaves of the South. It was a delicate balancing act that tested even Lincoln's light-footedness. This contemporary cartoon makes great play of Lincoln's humble background, not least a brief period as a laborer splitting rails.

THE RAIL CANDIDATE.

advantage, he was presiding over a war in which thousands were dying. How could slaughter on this scale ever be justified? He sustained himself by his belief that victory would result in the rebirth of the nation, thereby making these sacrifices worthwhile. He remained tormented, however, by the reality of the killing. Moral trials on this scale would try anyone. There were moments when, briefly, even Lincoln seemed to falter.

In the end he was proved right. The Union was saved, slavery was outlawed, and the great Republican experiment vindicated. Clearly, here was a man no one could write off as "typical."

All this said, leaving aside his exceptional height, Lincoln clearly embodied a number of typical American virtues of the period. He wasn't just humbly born but born into a frontier family for whom daily existence was a continuing struggle. The young Lincoln, whether chopping wood, drawing water, or going to bed hungry, was schooled early and hard. His mother's death in 1815, when he was only nine, would have seemed no more than an inevitable consequence of this frontier existence, one shared by thousands of the similarly struggling.

In these obviously unpromising circumstances, his almost complete lack of education was no more than could have been expected. Illiteracy in frontier Kentucky was a fact of life. Lincoln could hardly have hoped for anything different.

Except that, consistently, he did. Whether picking his delighted way through *Aesop's Fables* by candlelight in a Kentucky log cabin or confounding members of his cabinet in the Executive Mansion, Abraham Lincoln possessed a gift granted to few: not just moral certainty but an absolute determination to make it count.

Political Stirrings

1831–1842

Politics was always Abraham Lincoln's first love. His intellectual curiosity and voracious appetite for reading were largely satisfied by reading as many newspapers as possible. Given his father's example of civic and religious involvement, it is not difficult to see a young Abraham eager to make his mark on the world. Although he did not settle in New Salem, Illinois, until his return as a flatboat pilot in July 1831, he cast his first ballot in the August 1 election, voting for Edward Coles for Congress, Edmund Greer and Bowling Green to be magistrates, and Jack Armstrong and Henry Sinco for constables. The following year, he decided to run for the Illinois legislature, and placed eighth in a field of 13 candidates. Two years later, he ran again, this time winning a seat in the Illinois House of Representatives from Sangamon County.

Lincoln resided in what was often called the "Empire County"; before 1837, Sangamon was a county twice the size of the state of Rhode Island. Its inhabitants were a mixture of upland Southerners from Kentucky, Tennessee, and Virginia in addition to settlers from New England and Maryland. Sangamon was situated on some of the most fertile soil in the country, so farmers there made a good living. The population remained staunchly Whig, a political party created in 1834, throughout the period of the 1830s and 1840s. Because it was the most populous county in Illinois during the 1830s, it was represented by nine seats in the state legislature. The "Long Nine" of Sangamon County referred to the height of these representatives: most were at least six feet tall. Lincoln was the "longest of the Long Nine" at six feet four inches.

However, political stature was measured in more than physical height, and Abraham Lincoln seemed to win the respect of his fellow legislators quickly. John Todd Stuart, a leader in the Illinois general assembly, was one of the first to recognize his political and leadership skills. He helped gain a leadership role for Lincoln within the Whig Party caucus and became a political and personal mentor, suggesting that Lincoln read law. Because the legislature met on a biannual basis, meetings were infrequent, typically during the winter months when farmers did not have to tend to crops and lawyers did not have to attend court.

Lincoln served four consecutive terms in the Illinois legislature. During this time, he met the leading political and legal minds in Illinois, including Edward Dickinson Baker, John J. Hardin, Stephen A. Douglas, and Usher Linder. In 1837, Lincoln and the rest of the Long Nine were successful in relocating the seat of government from Vandalia to Springfield. Moving the capital farther north reflected the growth of population in the central and northern regions of Illinois, and proved to be an impetus to the continued prosperity of Springfield, bringing with it government contracts and support services. Construction of a new statehouse was shared by the state and the citizens of Springfield, who pledged to raise $50,000 for the structure and planned to complete it by the term commencing in December 1839. Lincoln was one of the leading citizens pledging to cover the portion for which Springfield was responsible.

Unfortunately, the statehouse was not finished in time for the beginning of the session, forcing the state representatives and senate to meet in local churches; representatives met in the Methodist Church. To prevent one particular bill from passing, the local Whigs boycotted the session to prevent the formation of a quorum—the number of members legally required to transact business. Lincoln stepped in to check the proceedings—only to have the door locked behind him. Democratic leaders had been keeping track of numbers and locked the door once a quorum had been reached. Lincoln and several other Whigs tried to prevent the vote by jumping out the window, but it was too late, and the vote went forward.

Lincoln served only one term in what is now called the Old State Capitol in Springfield. By 1842, he had his sights set on Congress.

OPPOSITE ABOVE Abraham Lincoln in the 1830s, when he first entered politics.

OPPOSITE BELOW A photograph of Stephen A. Douglas taken in the 1840s, around the time when Lincoln first met him.

RIGHT A political handbill distributed to Springfield voters.

BELOW The Old State Capitol in Spingfield, Illinois.

VOTING ON THE FRONTIER

Like most states, voting in Illinois was restricted to white males of 21 years or older. Literacy rates varied considerably on the Illinois frontier. Therefore *viva voca*, or "voice vote," was used to cast a ballot. Eligible voters went up to the election judge and indicated their selection for various offices. The election judge wrote down their selection in poll books, which were then filed with county clerks. Because politics was seen as a public activity and many people could neither read nor write, voice voting remained popular until 1848, when the new state constitution allowed for paper ballots.

Family Life

1842–1850

How did Abraham Lincoln overcome his awkwardness with women? He married a strong-willed, intelligent, attractive woman who also shared his ambition to succeed and a love of Whig politics. Mary Todd was the daughter of a successful Lexington, Kentucky, merchant and slave-owner, Robert Smith Todd. She was raised by black house slaves, sent to private schools, and grew up admiring Lexington's most notable resident, Henry Clay.

The death of her mother was a great blow to the young Mary, especially when her father quickly remarried and began raising a second family with his new bride. Mary and her sisters from the first marriage felt abandoned. When Elizabeth Todd, Mary's eldest sister, married a young lawyer, Ninian Wirt Edwards, Mary's life changed for the better. Elizabeth invited her sisters to spend time in their spacious Springfield, Illinois, home, which was located on what residents called "Aristocracy Hill." The Edwards gave elegant parties, inviting all the leading and up-and-coming men of the state. It was at

one of these events that Mary Todd met the shy, lanky Abraham Lincoln. In William Herndon's biography of Lincoln, the story is recounted of Lincoln asking Mary for a dance. "Miss Todd," he said, "I'd like to dance with you in the worst way." After the dance, Mary quipped, "He certainly did."

The courtship of Abraham Lincoln and Mary Todd was at times passionate, at times tender, and at other times stormy. An engagement was broken on January 1, 1841, a date that also marked the departure of Lincoln's closest friend, Joshua Fry Speed, from Springfield to Louisville, Kentucky. The letters Lincoln wrote to Speed reflect his inner doubts about marriage, yet the two lovers were eventually reconciled. Mary's own recollections claim that it was her authorship of an unsigned editorial attacking Illinois auditor James Shields that led to the reconciliation. When Shields, angered by the demeaning editorial, demanded to know who wrote it, Lincoln stepped forward and claimed credit for it. Shields challenged Lincoln to a duel; Lincoln accepted,

ABOVE A painting of Mary Todd Lincoln by her niece Katherine Helm.

LEFT A photograph of the Lincolns' Springfield home.

OPPOSITE RIGHT The tombstone of Lincoln's second son, Edward Baker Lincoln.

OPPOSITE LEFT Lincoln's youngest son, Thomas "Tad" Lincoln.

Thomas Lincoln

The second of four sons, Edward Baker Lincoln was named for Abraham Lincoln's political associate, Edward Dickinson Baker. Eddie, as he was known by his parents, was always sickly. In an age before antibiotics, children in the nineteenth century frequently succumbed to bacterial lung infections. On February 1, 1850, Eddie died of pulmonary tuberculosis, just short of his fourth birthday. His death emotionally devastated both parents. Mary looked for solace by joining the First Presbyterian Church. Abraham found comfort in religious discussions with the Reverend James Smith, who, like Lincoln himself, had been a religious skeptic early in his life.

but selected broadswords as weapons. Believing that he would be killed by pistols, Lincoln thought he had a height advantage with broadswords. Thankfully, he never found out: the duel, set for September 22 on Bloody Island, never took place because friends intervened to prevent it.

Abraham Lincoln and Mary Todd were married on November 4, 1842, in the parlor of the Edwards' home, and Mary gave birth to a son, Robert Todd Lincoln, on August 1, 1843. At the time, the Lincolns were renting a room at the Globe Tavern, a respectable Springfield inn. Baby Robert's crying forced them to rent a small cottage while searching for a permanent home. They eventually purchased a cottage from the Reverend Charles Dresser, the minister who had married them, and moved into their new home on May 1, 1844. That Lincoln

was able to pay cash for the home suggests that he was debt-free at the time. The couple had three more sons, although the second, Eddie, died in 1850.

Aside from Eddie's death, this period was probably the happiest for the Lincolns. They loved their children and indulged them in ways that gave them a reputation for being permissive parents. Mary read novels and poetry to the boys and encouraged their education. Abraham roughhoused with them when he was home, but his legal and political careers frequently took him away: on average, for six to nine months a year. In short, he was an absentee father, leaving the task of raising the boys and running the home to Mary. This led to conflict in Mary's life: she shared Lincoln's ambitions to succeed, but resented the time it took away from her.

Lincoln the Lawyer

1837-1859

It may seem odd to us that Abraham Lincoln struggled over the decision of whether to study law or become a blacksmith. At the time, blacksmiths were in great demand for the creation of all kinds of hardware, not just the shoeing of horses. In fact, by the end of the nineteenth century, many blacksmiths became proficient in the care and maintenance of "horseless carriages": automobiles.

Lincoln's decision to become a lawyer was based on many factors. As a literate man, he was often asked to write out legal forms for residents of New Salem who could neither read nor write; in fact, legal forms written in his hand exist from the years before he was a practicing attorney. By writing out legal forms for individuals, it gave Lincoln a taste for legal work and showed that people felt comfortable in letting him handle their affairs. His failed store with William Berry left him with a large debt, and he knew that knowledge of the law would help him navigate the complex legalities of his own circumstances.

Finally, he was encouraged by many of the great Illinois lawyers, especially John Todd Stuart.

Unless one studied at some of the older colleges on the Eastern seaboard or Transylvania College in Lexington, Kentucky, there were no standardized tests or requirements for becoming a lawyer. While there was a three-step process in Illinois, the most important training was simply to read and master basic legal texts, such as William Blackstone's *Commentaries*, Joseph Chitty's *Pleadings*, and Joseph Story's *Equity*. By the 1850s, it was also common for aspiring lawyers to apprentice in law firms.

John Todd Stuart took the young Lincoln in as a junior partner in 1837. Stuart's election to Congress in 1838 left Lincoln alone to tend to business. Initially, he welcomed the change, as illustrated by his entry in the firm's account book, "Commencement of Lincoln's administration." Yet it soon became clear that he required more

BECOMING A LAWYER

Formal schools for training lawyers did not exist on the Illinois frontier; there were no standardized tests for becoming an attorney. Rather, testing by practicing attorneys could amount to a rigorous oral exam of the law or simply being treated to a good dinner with drinks. Individuals interested in becoming a lawyer began by reading law books. For men like Lincoln, the first step in becoming an attorney was to have your name entered on the Sangamon circuit court record as a person of good moral character. The second was to be issued with a license to practice law in all courts of the state by justices of the Illinois Supreme Court. The final step was to have your name entered on the roll of attorneys in the office of the clerk of the Illinois Supreme Court.

mentoring in the law. Stephen Trigg Logan, one of the great legal minds in Illinois, took him under his wing in 1841, and for the next three years, Lincoln learned from a master lawyer. In 1844, he decided to set up his own practice and took as his junior partner William Henry Herndon, whose family he knew from New Salem.

The project "The Papers of Abraham Lincoln" seeks to make available all letters sent to Lincoln and all documents written by Lincoln. Until the project workers scoured the Illinois county courthouses and the appellate and federal court records, much of the information on Lincoln's legal career consisted of little more than anecdotes from fellow attorneys and accounts of a few famous cases. Myths arose which claimed that Lincoln was not very informed about the law and used his folksy charm to win over juries, that he only took cases he felt were morally just, or that he was a railroad lawyer. All myths contain a kernel of truth, but they tend to be exaggerated. What is known is that Lincoln's legal practice was large for his time. He seems to have been a workaholic who spent time preparing cases based upon legal precedents that were readily available in the law library in the statehouse. Undoubtedly, Lincoln also subscribed to the major law journals of the day.

He did not specialize in any particular type of law but took cases as they presented themselves. Of the cases Lincoln handled regarding railroads, a small portion of his practice, 50 percent were on behalf of the railroad and the other half were parties suing railroads for relief. If there can be any generalizations about his legal practice, then it is that Lincoln believed all people deserved to have their day in court and to have their interests represented in the best manner possible—regardless of their guilt or innocence.

In the 1830s and 1840s, it was impossible to be a successful lawyer simply by waiting for business. It was necessary to travel the judicial circuit to the various county courthouses and solicit business. Lincoln lived in the Eighth Judicial Circuit headed by Judge David Davis of Bloomington, Illinois. The court calendar, which consisted of three months in the spring and three months in the fall, took Lincoln away from home for six months on average.

OPPOSITE ABOVE William Henry Herndon, Lincoln's law partner from 1844.

OPPOSITE BELOW The law office of Lincoln on Fifth Street in Springfield.

ABOVE RIGHT Lincoln arguing an early legal case in New Salem.

LEFT The shaving mirror Lincoln used when traveling on the judicial circuit.

Congressman Lincoln

1843–1849

Illinois's Seventh Congressional District was largely populated by Whigs, making it a safe seat for any Whig politician. As a number of ambitious Whig leaders came forward, serving in Congress became a point of contention within the party. The three leading Whig contenders were John J. Hardin, Edward Dickinson Baker, and Abraham Lincoln. At the 1843 party convention, Hardin was selected as the congressional candidate with a resolution that Baker should be considered at the next election. Baker was duly nominated in 1844 and served his term in Congress. Lincoln assumed he would get the nomination for the 1846 election, but was taken aback when Hardin declared that he was again running for the seat. Citing that "Turn about is fair play," Lincoln was able to secure the nomination.

Peter Cartwright, a famed Methodist minister in central Illinois, ran against Lincoln for the congressional seat. Lincoln disliked Cartwright, claiming that he mixed too much politics into his preaching. Cartwright began a whispering campaign right before the election which suggested that Lincoln was not a believer and mocked organized religion. Lincoln responded with a printed statement acknowledging that he was "not a member of any Christian Church," but that he "never denied the truth of the Scriptures." He won easily, with 6,340 votes to Cartwright's 4,829.

Lincoln decided to take his family with him to Washington. They rented their Springfield home to Cornelius Ludlum, a brick contractor, and stopped en route in Lexington, Kentucky, to visit Mary's family before continuing to the capital. Mrs. Sprigg, a widow who lived near the Capitol building, rented rooms to the Lincolns. When the two younger boys, Robert and Eddie, made too much noise for the new congressman, Mary returned with them to Lexington. As soon as she left, Lincoln regretted the decision and missed Mary's company.

Like most new congressmen, Lincoln's term was undistinguished. He introduced a series of resolutions criticizing President James K. Polk and his Mexican-American War (1846–1848) policy. Because he demanded that Polk show the spot where American blood had been shed on American soil, Lincoln's critics soon referred to him as "Spotty Abe." Like most Whigs, Lincoln criticized the war yet voted for military supplies for the soldiers. He also tried to introduce an amendment to a resolution for abolishing slavery in the District of Columbia through compensated emancipation. Lacking support, however, the

BLUEPRINT FOR SUCCESS

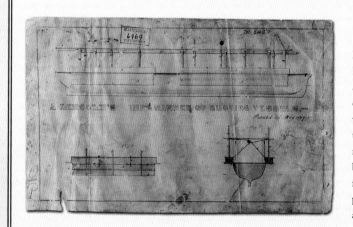

Lincoln had a passion for inventions and technology. Drawing upon his experience with the sandbars in the Sangamon River, he invented a device to lift boats over obstacles. Bellows on either side of the boat would be lowered and inflated, carrying the boat over the obstruction. Although the invention was never manufactured, Lincoln remains the only U.S. president to be awarded a patent: he received Patent #6469 for "A Device for Buoying Vessels Over Shoals" on May 22, 1849. As president, he loved to walk through the U.S. Patent Office and look at the glass cases containing models of inventions.

ABOVE A colored lithograph of the Capitol in Washington, D.C., in 1848.

LEFT The diagram for Abraham Lincoln's patent, 1849.

amendment was never introduced. When John Quincy Adams collapsed from a stroke on the floor of the House of Representatives in February 1848 (he died two days later), a congressional committee was formed to plan the memorial observances, and Lincoln was a member of the committee.

When Zachary Taylor was elected president in 1848, Lincoln hoped for a federal appointment. He sought a position in the commission of the Land Office, but lost out to a Chicago lawyer, Justin Butterfield. When asked if he opposed the Mexican-American War, Butterfield replied: "No, by God. I oppose no wars. I opposed one war [the War of 1812], and it ruined me, and henceforth I am for War, Pestilence and Famine." As a concession, Lincoln was offered the governorship of the Oregon Territory, an appointment he turned down.

Abraham Lincoln had achieved his goal of serving in Congress, and thus focused on rebuilding his law practice once he returned to Springfield. His political thirst seemed to have been quenched for the time being–until the Kansas-Nebraska Act reignited his ambitions.

LEFT Winfield Scott, general in the U.S. Army during the war with Mexico.

BELOW The Siege of Veracruz, which took place from March 9–29, 1847, during the Mexican-American War. The United States force under General Winfield Scott was the first large-scale amphibious assault conducted by the United States military. It ended with the surrender and occupation of Veracruz by the United States. As a congressman, Lincoln was critical of the war.

The Crisis of the 1850s

The election of Andrew Jackson as president in 1828 had ushered in a new era of politics. Using Jackson's charismatic personality, Martin Van Buren, a New York politician, created the modern Democratic Party structure. Opponents of "King Andrew" eventually organized themselves into the opposition party using the term "Whig," which was associated with anti-monarchical sentiments during the American Revolution. These parties were national in character, replacing regional factions and coalitions. The historian Daniel Walker Howe in *The American Whigs* described the differences: "The Whigs proposed a society that would be economically diverse but culturally uniform; the Democrats preferred economic uniformity but were more tolerant of cultural and moral diversity."

Two factors undermined the two-party rule established by Democrats and Whigs. The first was that slavery remained an unresolved issue. The Declaration of Independence (1776), reflecting the natural rights doctrine of the Enlightenment, declared that "all men are created equal," intimating that equality was not something given by men or governments but an innate right, placing it beyond men to give or take away. The Constitution (1789) that followed it, however, was a dry document which placed limits on power and defended property rights. Slaves were considered property. The contradiction between the inherent humanity of slaves and their everyday treatment in some states as mere property, and thus lacking any rights, challenged the best political minds of the age. A series of compromises

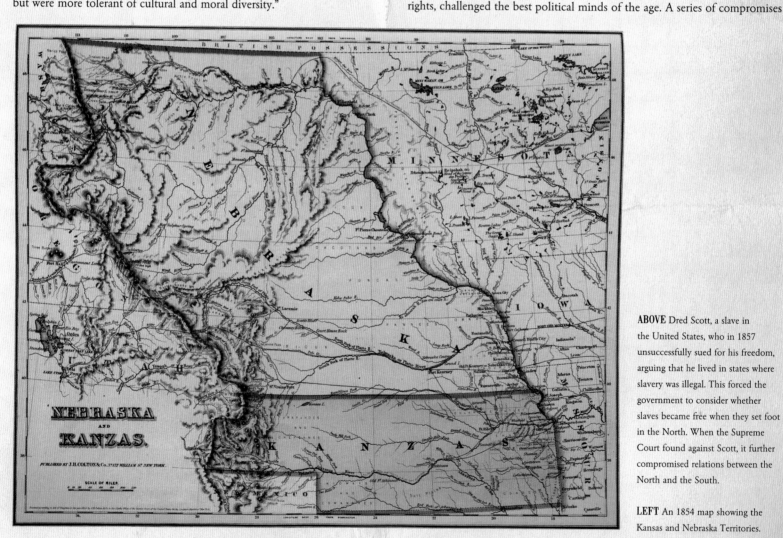

ABOVE Dred Scott, a slave in the United States, who in 1857 unsuccessfully sued for his freedom, arguing that he lived in states where slavery was illegal. This forced the government to consider whether slaves became free when they set foot in the North. When the Supreme Court found against Scott, it further compromised relations between the North and the South.

LEFT An 1854 map showing the Kansas and Nebraska Territories.

tried to provide concessions to slaveholders as well as to a growing opposition to slavery and its extension into U.S. territories.

The second factor was the increase of foreign immigration into the United States. Irish and Germans made up the largest immigrant populations. Many Protestant Americans were threatened by the influx of Catholics, who were seen as harboring unsound beliefs. In 1849, a secret organization called the Order of the Star-Spangled Banner was created in New York City, in opposition to the perceived threat of foreigners taking over the country. Soon its members appeared in major cities across the nation.

The Democratic Party began to fracture during the 1850s over the slavery issue. In 1854, Stephen A. Douglas, in an attempt to settle the western lands rapidly, introduced a series of measures collectively known as the Kansas-Nebraska Bill. It effectively removed the 1820 Missouri Compromise line establishing the boundaries of slavery. Douglas embraced "popular sovereignty," a doctrine that left the decision about slavery up to the citizens of the territories. Many Northern anti-slavery Democrats objected and split from the party. The Kansas Territory became torn between forces opposed to slavery and those who supported it. Prior to statehood, two different state constitutions were created: one supporting slavery and one opposing it. President James Buchanan recognized the pro-slavery, or Lecompton, constitution. This led Stephen A. Douglas, a member of President Buchanan's own party, to split openly with his administration.

The final element of the crisis was the rapid disappearance of the Whig Party. The emergence of new parties such as the Know-Nothing and Republican Parties peeled off large portions of Whigs. By the election of 1856, the Whig Party lacked a presidential candidate and national organization.

JOHN BROWN

Meeting the Slave mother and her Child on the steps of Charlestown jail on his way to execution

The Artist has represented Capt. Brown re... ...sor, a Slave-mother and Child who obstructed the passage on his way to the Scaffold... ...kissed the Child then...

THE KNOW-NOTHINGS

The American Party emerged out of the Order of the Star-Spangled Banner in the 1850s in opposition to the Democratic Party, which openly embraced foreign immigrants as party members. The American Party members were often referred to as Know-Nothings by opponents because members were instructed to reply to questions about party business with the phrase "I know nothing." Know-Nothings had some success in local and regional elections but never at the national level. At first, Lincoln thought this movement would be short-lived, but its persistence throughout the 1850s convinced him that Know-Nothing voters needed to be recruited to his side— regardless of their principles.

ABOVE John Brown, an American abolitionist who believed in armed insurrection to end slavery. He led the Pottawatomie massacre in 1856 in Kansas in which five pro-slavery Southerners were killed. In 1859 he led the raid on the federal armory at Harpers Ferry, West Virginia, with the intention of arming slaves. This raid escalated the tensions that would lead to secession and the Civil War two years later.

LEFT A meeting of the Know-Nothing Party in New York City.

Slavery and Abolitionists

Whatever the moral repugnance slavery may have generated across much of the North, a repugnance that was certainly shared by Lincoln despite his cautious public statements, it lay at the economic heart of the Southern states. Without it, the South could never have survived, let alone prospered. It was its lifeblood. By a considerable margin, slaves were the single largest asset in the country, worth more, at least on paper, than all the banks, railroads, and emerging industries of the North put together. On the eve of the Civil War, the total value of the four million slaves in the United States, the overwhelming majority in the South, was $3.5 billion.

Both their numbers and their value had grown sharply since 1800. The invention of the cotton gin (a machine that rapidly separated cotton fibers from their seeds) in 1793 allied to the rapid westward expansion not only dramatically increased agricultural production but made it possible for cotton, alongside other staples such as tobacco, rice, and sugar, to be grown economically in the new western lands: in Tennessee and Kentucky, thereafter in Alabama, Georgia, Mississippi, Arkansas, Louisiana, and Texas. Over this period, the average value of an individual slave increased almost threefold: from $300 in 1800 to $800 in 1860, though a healthy young male slave could fetch as much as $5,000. The slave trade itself may have been outlawed by the United States in 1808—though an illegal trade certainly continued—but an enforced internal mass migration of 600,000 slaves to the new lands took place.

But slavery to the South was always more than a matter of economics. It was critical to the South's self-identity and self-worth, underpinning a society that was vigorously self-confident and acutely conscious of its role in the birth of the United States. In a world otherwise becoming mechanized and soulless, the South reveled in its gallant past and its rapidly expanding agricultural future.

There was no shortage of those determined to sustain this startlingly unequal world. Far from seeing slavery as obviously inhumane and impossible to reconcile with Christian values, James Hammond, governor of South Carolina and subsequently the state's senator, asserted, "American slavery is not only not a sin, but especially commanded by God through Moses, and approved by Christ through his apostles." The Virginian George Fitzhugh, claiming that "the negro is but a grown-up child," argued that slavery benefited blacks, comparing their working conditions favorably to those of oppressed if free factory workers in the North. But most crucially of all, the South could point not just to the constitutional right to own slaves but to that of any state to determine the legality or otherwise of slavery in its own borders. After all, George Washington and Thomas Jefferson had both been slave owners. Put simply, slavery was legal.

Southern intransigence on this scale served only to harden attitudes among the abolitionists of the North, as, perhaps paradoxically, did those attempts to find a lasting solution to the problem. The Fugitive Slave Act of 1850, which gave federal commissioners the right to arrest and return to the South escaped slaves, caused outrage in the North, as did the Supreme Court's *Dred Scott* decision in 1857, which ruled that even in non-slave states, slaves could not demand their freedom as this would deprive their owners of legally held property.

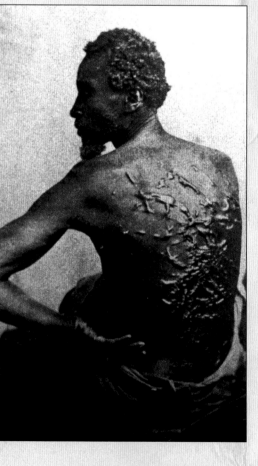

ABOVE Frederick Douglass in a photograph made later in life. He spoke publicly and published a newspaper pushing for full equality of African Americans before and during the war.

RIGHT An adult male displays welts on his back, the result of multiple beatings. This ex-slave escaped during the war and served in the Union army.

OPPOSITE ABOVE Slaves separating cotton on the Smith plantation in Virginia. The cotton gin and other advancements in processing the fiber did not reduce the producers' use of slave labor.

In this overheated atmosphere, speeches, pamphlets, newspaper articles, books, and political rallies proliferated, all adding to the clamor for the abolition of slavery. Ex-slaves such as Frederick Douglass and Sojourner Truth were willingly pressed into service in the abolitionist cause. Harriet Beecher Stowe's 1852 novel, *Uncle Tom's Cabin*, about an elderly and much put-upon slave sustained by his Christian faith, similarly provided critical impetus to the abolitionists, becoming the best-selling book of the entire nineteenth century.

The Underground Railroad, an informal network of safe houses and clandestine routes manned at considerable personal risk by abolitionist volunteers, was active in smuggling slaves to safety. No reliable numbers of how many slaves escaped on the Underground Railroad exist: estimates vary between 30,000 and 100,000. It seems probable that even at its peak between 1850 and 1860 only about 1,000 slaves a year were spirited to freedom. It is arguable that the railroad harmed rather than helped many slaves, provoking slave owners, whose loathing of it was limitless, to guard their slaves all the more strictly. Douglass, for one, believed that the publicity it enjoyed may have been useful in drawing attention to the abolitionist crusade to smash slavery but that it did little to ease the plight of the slaves themselves. The existence of the Underground Railroad was also one of the prime reasons the South pushed so strenuously for the passing of the Fugitive Slave Act.

Slavery is the corner-stone of our republican edifice

Govenor McDuffie, governor of South Carolina 1834–36

ANTHONY BURNS

Anthony Burns was a Virginia-born slave who in 1853 escaped from the South, making his way by ship to Boston. The following year, he was recognized, arrested, and, under the terms of the Fugitive Slave Act, forcibly returned to his owner, Charles F. Suttle. The case caused pandemonium in Boston, enormously strengthening the abolitionist ranks. Those Bostonians who had recognized the need for compromise with the South almost overnight became rabid abolitionists. It also brought chaos to the streets of the city as vast crowds, amid considerable violence, marched to demand the release of Burns. For Northerners by the millions, what seemed to them the evident injustice of such cases inevitably stirred passions to the point where, in the end, war seemed not just probable but necessary.

ABOVE After his enforced return to the South, Burns was purchased by abolitionists in Boston, who then freed him. He later moved to Canada, where he became a Baptist preacher. He died in 1862, aged 28, from tuberculosis.

The Birth of the Republican Party

1852-1856

Following his return from Congress, Lincoln threw all of his energies into his law practice. He gave some political speeches during the 1852 presidential campaign, but politics no longer excited his passion. This changed with the passage of the Kansas-Nebraska Act in 1854. Lincoln had never liked slavery but was willing to accept it as the price for maintaining the Union; thus, his opposition to the Kansas-Nebraska Act was its removal of all barriers limiting slavery's expansion. The Missouri Compromise had set a firm, defined line between slavery and freedom extending across the territories. The removal of this line not only reopened the issue in the territories, Lincoln also believed that it meant nothing could prevent Stephen A. Douglas's doctrine of popular sovereignty from being invoked in free states to reintroduce slavery.

Abraham Lincoln had always been a Whig in politics. With the decline of the Whig Party, he found himself without a party to represent his opposition to Democratic Party measures. Joshua Fry Speed, Lincoln's closest friend, inquired if he had joined the Know-Nothing Party. Lincoln replied:

I am not a Know-Nothing. That is certain. How could I be? How can anyone who abhors the oppression of negroes, be in favor of degrading classes of white people? Our progress in degeneracy appears to me to be pretty rapid. As a nation, we began by declaring that "all men are created equal." We now practically read it "all men are created equal, except negroes." When the Know-Nothings get control, it will read "all men are created equal, except negroes, and foreigners, and catholics." When it comes to this I should prefer to emigrate to some country where they make no pretence of loving liberty—to Russia, for instance, where despotism can be taken pure, and without the base alloy of hypocrisy.

In this letter Lincoln also professed to remain a Whig even though he admitted "others say there are no Whigs." He ran for the United States Senate seat in 1855 but threw his support behind Lyman Trumbull, an antislavery Democrat. This prevented a "Douglas Democrat," Joel Matteson, from obtaining the seat. Lincoln and Trumbull shared common ground on preventing the expansion of slavery.

Lincoln's hesitancy in joining the Republican Party was based upon practical considerations. In Illinois, the Republicans had yet to organize throughout the state. This changed in February 1856, with the call for a state convention to meet in Bloomington. Lincoln attended this convention on May 29 and gave a speech so rousing that reporters allegedly forgot to take notes. The convention endorsed a slate of candidates and drafted a platform. As a recognized leader of the Illinois Republican Party, Lincoln worked to change the public perception of Republicans as rabid abolitionists—those who wanted the immediate end of slavery—to the more moderate view of

ABRAHAM LINCOLN: VICE PRESIDENT?

The first Republican National Convention met in Philadelphia, Pennsylvania, from June 1–19, 1856. John C. Frémont was the overwhelming favorite for nomination as presidential candidate, but the nomination for vice-presidential candidate was divided among 15 men. William L. Dayton of New Jersey had 253 votes, the largest total in an informal ballot, with Abraham Lincoln receiving the second-largest at 110, and Nathaniel P. Banks of Massachusetts coming in a poor third with just 46. The convention united around Dayton by acclamation. Lincoln, who did not attend, initially thought the 110 votes were for Ezra Lincoln, a delegate from Boston, Massachusetts.

an anti-slavery party: those who wanted the eventual elimination of slavery over time but desired an immediate prevention of its expansion into the territories.

When John C. Frémont was nominated as the Republican presidential candidate, Lincoln worked hard in Illinois for his election. He realized that the only way Frémont could win would be to convince the Know-Nothings that their interests lay in supporting him. Lincoln worked to fuse various elements of old Whigs, anti-slavery Democrats, and Know-Nothings into the Republican camp. The Republicans made important gains in Illinois when their candidates were elected as governor and secretary of state; thus Lincoln realized that the political momentum in Illinois favored the Republicans.

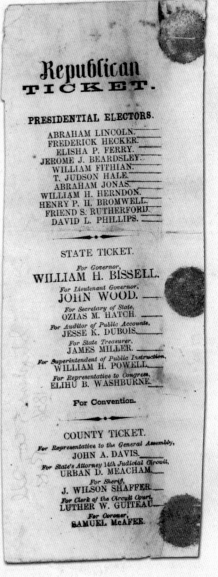

OPPOSITE Abraham Lincoln in 1857.

ABOVE LEFT U.S. Representative Norman Buel Judd from Illinois. He was a member of the Illinois Senate from 1844 to 1860, a delegate to the 1860 Republican National Convention, and Lincoln made him Minister Plenipotentiary to Berlin in March 1861.

LEFT William Henry Bissell, the governor of Illinois from 1857 to 1860 and one of the first Republican candidates to achieve success in an election.

ABOVE RIGHT An 1856 political ticket featuring Lincoln on the ballot.

The 1860 Election Debates

During the 1800s, the issue of slavery began to erode the unity of the nation. National mediating institutions divided along sectional lines, mainstream Protestant churches split along North/South regional divides, and national political parties fractured over slavery. Even the Supreme Court became discredited with the March 1857 *Dred Scott v. Sandford* decision. At the same time, the court also declared that the 1820 Missouri Compromise was unconstitutional—a decision that cleared the way for allowing slavery in all of the country's territories.

The Illinois 1858 U.S. senatorial election pitted Abraham Lincoln against Stephen A. Douglas. As in most states at the time, senators in Illinois were elected by the legislature, not by a direct election of the voters. Lincoln delivered a rousing speech in June at the statehouse, drawing on a biblical reference from the book of Matthew, when he said that "a house divided against itself cannot stand." The country, he said, could not remain half slave and half free. Eastern Republican newspaper editors, meanwhile, began to urge Illinois voters to reelect Douglas.

Douglas believed in the issue of popular sovereignty, but Lincoln thought this a dangerous policy and sought to show that Douglas did not represent Republican interests. He challenged the senator to a series of public debates that resulted in what are now called the seven Lincoln-Douglas debates. Each debate lasted three hours, with an hour opening statement by one candidate, a one-and-a-half-hour answer by the other, and a 30-minute rebuttal. The speaking order alternated at each debate site.

Douglas continued to advance his doctrine of popular sovereignty, claiming that he did not care if slavery were voted up or down. Feeding upon the racial fears among white voters, Douglas painted Lincoln as an abolitionist who demanded immediate black equality and interracial marriage. While Lincoln continued to claim that slaves were entitled to the rights granted to "men" in the Declaration of Independence, he denied being an abolitionist, saying instead that he opposed the expansion of slavery into the territories. He also argued that, with the passing of the Kansas-Nebraska Act and the *Dred Scott* decision, Democrats were conspiring to nationalize slavery.

The debates received national attention because of Douglas's stature as the likely Democratic presidential candidate in 1860. Even though Lincoln lost the senate seat, he had held his own against Douglas in front of a national audience. Compiling newspaper accounts of the debates, Lincoln published them in 1860, and over 30,000 copies sold during the course of

SPEECH

OF

HON. ABRAM LINCOLN,

BEFORE THE

REPUBLICAN STATE CONVENTION,

June 16, 1858.

"The result is not doubtful. We shall not fail—if we stand firm, we shall not fail."

Sycamore.
O. P. BASSETT, PR., TRUE REPUBLICAN OFFICE.
1858.

ABOVE The first printing of Abraham Lincoln's "House Divided" speech.

a few months. With the 1860 presidential campaign came the fracturing of the Democratic Party. It split along regional lines between Douglas, who represented the northern wing, and John Breckinridge, who represented the southern wing. Both Douglas and Breckinridge ran under separate party banners. At the Republican Convention in Chicago, Illinois, Lincoln was able to beat three other better-known contenders for the nomination. Finally, another Southerner, John Bell, ran as a Constitutional Union candidate. The fact that Lincoln's name did not even appear on ballots in most Southern states further added to the sectional character of the election. The electoral math indicated that if the Republicans could carry the Northern states, they would win the election, which they did, making Abraham Lincoln the first Republican president of the United States. The result only served to feed Southern fears that slavery continued to be threatened in spite of Lincoln's reassurances that he desired only to prevent the spread of slavery into the territories that did not already have it, not its immediate abolition.

ABOVE A 1919 painting of Lincoln and Stephen A. Douglas during a debate at Charleston, Illinois, on September 18, 1858.

RIGHT The August 8, 1860, campaign rally held outside Lincoln's home.

ON THE HUSTINGS

Young men turning voting age were actively recruited into "Wide Awake Clubs," so called because of the need to be alert to opposition-party tricks. For the largest political rally ever witnessed in Springfield on August 8, 1860, the Republican Party recruited bands and Wide Awake Clubs from across Illinois to attend. The parade began at 10 a.m. and continued until 2 p.m., passing in front of Abraham Lincoln's home on its way to the fairgrounds west of the city. Floats, one with a log cabin upon it, were present in abundance. The afternoon was filled with prominent speakers, and the evening found Springfield's streets overflowing with thousands of Wide Awakes marching in a flashlight procession.

The Union Dissolved

April 12, 1861, was the day the United States ceased to be one nation united, and embarked on a four-year civil war. The previous December, South Carolina had seceded from the Union, and in the next few months, six other Southern states joined together to form a confederacy in which state sovereignty reigned. On April 12, South Carolina exercised that sovereignty by opening fire on Federal government property in Charleston Harbor, Fort Sumter.

The tension between North and South that led to secession and the formation of the Confederate States of America went back more than half a century. Since the early part of the nineteenth century, the agrarian states of the South had come under increasing fire for their use of slave labor. As the young country expanded westward, abolitionists and others in the North tried to limit the spread of slavery. Starting with the Missouri Compromise of 1820 and continuing to the brink of the Civil War, congressional action created interim settlements that quickly broke down.

The first shot in the conflict was symbolically fired in November of 1860 with the election of Abraham Lincoln as president. Lincoln, representing the new anti-slavery Republican Party, gained nationwide fame with his eloquent speeches and debates denouncing slavery. Lincoln had in fact no intention of abolishing slavery in the South when he took office, but South Carolina interpreted his election as a sign of the increasing shift of Federal political power away from the pro-slavery South. The citizens of Charleston began

harassment of the U.S. Army garrison stationed at Fort Moultrie in Charleston Harbor, which, together with Castle Pinckney, about a mile off the waterfront, and Fort Sumter, at the mouth of the harbor, represented the Federal military presence in the city.

The newly arrived commander of the three forts was Major Robert Anderson. He quickly assessed the situation and made urgent requests to Washington for supplies and reinforcements. Little help came from President James Buchanan, a weak, lame-duck figure who wished to delay the crisis until after he left office, or Secretary of War John Floyd, a Southerner sympathetic to secession. Lacking a definitive order to defend Fort Moultrie against the secessionists, Anderson moved its garrison to Fort Sumter on the evening of December 26, 1860.

Even though Anderson viewed the move to Fort Sumter as one to delay confrontation, Southerners viewed the appearance of the Stars and Stripes over the fort as an act of aggression. By the time Lincoln took the oath of office on March 4, 1861, the construction of the Charleston batteries under the command of Brigadier General Pierre Gustave Toutant Beauregard was nearly complete. "We are not enemies, but friends. We must not be enemies," Lincoln implored in his inaugural address. But it was too late for conciliation. Anderson was running out of supplies, and to relieve him, a mission would have to be sent to Fort Sumter.

OPPOSITE ABOVE Abraham Lincoln's direct involvement in the Civil War was crucial to eventual Union victory.

LEFT A lithograph of Fort Sumter as it looked in 1861.

OPPOSITE BELOW Federal guns fire from inside Fort Sumter in this period lithograph. The fort was designed to defend against ships entering Charleston Harbor, so most of the cannons inside the fort had limited effect against the rebel shore batteries.

WARTIME LEADER

In many ways, Abraham Lincoln was as instrumental in saving the Union as the battlefield victories of the North. He may have peered too far as commander in chief into the day-to-day activities of the military, but his instincts in that direction were valid. He was able to evaluate talent and apply just enough pressure on those generals who had what it took, while replacing those who did not. In handling the delicate political situation during the war, Lincoln had no equal.

The newly chosen head of the Confederate government, former Mississippi senator Jefferson Davis, convened his cabinet in Montgomery, Alabama, and together they concluded that Fort Sumter must not be resupplied. Any other position would have risked a loss of faith in the new government.

On April 11, Beauregard received word from Montgomery to deliver a surrender ultimatum to Anderson. Former South Carolina senator James Chesnut, now a colonel on Beauregard's staff, was charged with delivering the message. He and several other officers rowed out to the fort. Anderson declined to surrender, but he hinted to Chesnut that without supplies the Federal garrison might soon be forced to give up the fort. This "rowboat" diplomacy dragged on into the early hours of the 12th, as each side sought to avoid firing the first shot. Finally, at 3:30 a.m., Chesnut informed Anderson that bombardment of the fort would commence in one hour. A cannon was then readied to give the signal for the firing to begin. The lanyard was offered to outspoken secessionist Roger Pryor, but he declined to pull it. So Lieutenant Henry Farley did, at 4:30 a.m. on April 12, 1861.

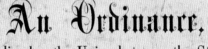

An Ordinance,

To dissolve the Union between the State of South Carolina and other States united with her under the compact entitled, "The Constitution of the United States of America."

We, the People of the State of South Carolina, in Convention assembled, do declare and ordain, and it is hereby declared and ordained,

That the Ordinance adopted by us in Convention, on the twenty-third day of May, in the year of our Lord one thousand seven hundred and eighty-eight, whereby the Constitution of the United States of America was ratified, and also, all Acts and parts of Acts of the General Assembly of this State, ratifying amendments of the said Constitution, are hereby repealed; and that the union now subsisting between South Carolina and other States, under the name of "The United States of America," is hereby dissolved.

EVANS & COGSWELL, PRINTERS, CHARLESTON.

JEFFERSON DAVIS

Davis was a reluctant president of the Confederacy, but having accepted the job, he performed it with gusto. A West Point graduate and former Secretary of War, he at times micromanaged the military, clashing frequently with his top generals. He often sought the advice of General Robert E. Lee, who advised him on strategy and resource management. Like Lincoln, Davis had to contend with a legislature that was frequently divided and "political generals," whose agendas rarely had the good of the state as their first priority.

The batteries around the harbor joined in and for several hours received no answering fire from Fort Sumter. When the Federals finally opened fire at about 7:00 a.m., their solid shot, meant for sinking an invading armada, did little damage to the well-protected Confederate guns. A squadron of ships sent to resupply the fort began to arrive off the Charleston bar shortly before the start of the bombardment, but planning errors, indecision, and poor sea conditions prevented any of the supplies from reaching Sumter. The fort, meanwhile, was holding up reasonably well, having withstood more than 3,000 shots. However, fires in the fort's wooden buildings, mostly from heated cannonballs lobbed into the interior by mortars, created difficult and dangerous conditions for the garrison. An honorable surrender was worked out between Anderson and Beauregard's representatives before the 33-hour bombardment ended.

Ironically, the only two fatalities on either side occurred accidentally during Anderson's parting cannon salute to the U.S. flag. The Federal garrison left Charleston on the resupply ships and a telegraph dispatch informed Lincoln and the nation of Fort Sumter's surrender and the end of peace in an undivided union.

OPPOSITE LEFT As this commemorative copy of South Carolina's ordinance of secession illustrates, leaders there believed that the United States Constitution was a contract that individual states could break.

OPPOSITE RIGHT A photograph of Jefferson Davis, the president of the Confederacy.

RIGHT This illustration of Fort Sumter on fire was created by an African American who observed the April 12, 1861, bombardment.

BELOW The bombardment of Fort Sumter in full swing, April 12, 1861.

Opening Salvos: Fort Sumter and Bull Run

APRIL 12–JULY 21, 1861

Deftly enticed by Lincoln, at 4:30 in the afternoon of April 12, 1861, the Confederacy began the bombardment of Fort Sumter in Charleston Bay, South Carolina. These were the first shots of the Civil War. Fort Sumter, one of a string of military strongpoints dotted along the Atlantic coast of the United States, had been built in the War of 1812 to repulse British attacks on America's eastern seaboard. In 1861, it was one of a number of Federal military posts that now found themselves in enemy territory.

In these first, tentative days of the war, Fort Sumter assumed an ominous significance. Its 127-man garrison needed to be resupplied. What was once a routine operation now threatened a continent-wide conflict. For the Confederates, any such resupply by the North would represent an act of obvious aggression. For the Unionists, failure to resupply Fort Sumter would be tantamount to a surrender of its authority. Lincoln, precisely aware of the consequences of his decision, ordered the fort resupplied.

As the Federal fleet entered Charleston Bay, the land-based Confederate batteries opened up. They fired more or less continuously for almost 36 hours. With the fort's own artillery designed to resist a seaborne invasion, it had no effective response. It surrendered the following day. The garrison was then courteously allowed to return to the North. There were three deaths, one Confederate, two Union. Compared to the savage fighting to come, not least the North's repeated attempts to seize Charleston two years later, it seemed almost decorous. But Lincoln had made his point: the South had fired first.

There was a similar sense of misplaced gallantry when, in July, the North launched its first major land assault on the Confederacy. The result, the First Battle of Bull Run (or First Manassas as it was known in the South) was a dismayingly bloody and humiliating defeat for the North. Yet even in Confederate ranks, victory made plain a lesson no one could ignore: that this was to be a conflict of a ferocity no one had anticipated, one in which hopes of swift and glorious victory would play no part.

ABOVE The Stone House on the Warrenton Turnpike was in the path of the Federal advance. It acted as a hospital during the First Battle of Bull Run, and still stands today.

OPPOSITE The Confederacy bombards Fort Sumter, a key Federal stronghold, on April 12, 1861, signaling the start of the Civil War.

ABOVE The capture at Bull Run of Captain James D. Ricketts's battery by the 33rd Virginia infantry. These guns and another Federal battery were captured and recaptured throughout the day.

BELOW Railroads transformed war, allowing men and matériel to be moved faster and in larger numbers than ever before.

Yet swift victory was precisely what had prompted the Union attack. Lincoln himself was its prime mover. Desperate for an early demonstration of Union martial vigor, dismayed by the snail-like caution of the Union commander, General Irvin McDowell, and actuely aware of the numerical superiority of the Union forces, Lincoln cajoled, demanded, and pleaded with McDowell for a Union attack. He was no less conscious that forward elements of the Confederate troops were within 25 miles of Washington.

The battle was the largest fought in North America to date, 35,000 Union forces against perhaps 22,000 Confederates. Against a brittle background of cries of "On to Richmond" and with Washington high society decamping en masse to vantage points around the battlefield with picnics and parasols to revel in the presumed Union triumph, the Union forces were routed, fleeing in disarray after their early gains were reversed. Hundreds were taken prisoner. Federal casualties were 3,000, Confederate losses 1,750. Almost the only

Northern consolation was that the exhausted Confederates were then unable to press home their advantage. Humiliated, the Union army crept northward. For Lincoln and the North, it was a somber day.

The keys to the Confederate victory had been partly their readiness to improvise, with troops deployed with greater certainty than the Union's more ponderous commanders seemed capable of; partly a more obvious fighting spirit. Given that they were fighting in defense of their own lands, their superior willingness to engage the enemy may seem understandable. Yet for Lincoln this hardly excused McDowell's shortcomings. He was fired within days.

A disturbing pattern was emerging for the North, soon to repeat itself on a much larger scale: whatever its superior material resources, it was confronting not just better fighting troops but better-led troops. For Lincoln, the outlook could hardly have been more unpromising.

RAILROADS IN THE CIVIL WAR

The military use of railroads is among the reasons why the Civil War is considered the first modern war. Dramatic troop movements, such as those at First Manassas, illustrated the possibilities of rapid deployment, but supplies were the principal cargo. Troops on both sides could expect to march many a long and dusty mile. Railroads were vulnerable to raids and sabotage. The South had additional problems: varying track gauges and scarcity of replacement parts. Both North and South also had to contend with the demands of independent railroad companies. As a result, in 1862 the North established a military rail system.

Civil War Forces and Strategies

1861–1865

The Civil War was different from earlier nineteenth-century conflicts. The two enemies spoke the same language, and shared a similar—if not identical—heritage. It was a war that truly pitted brother against brother. As a result, in the beginning both sides believed that swift victory would lead to a cessation of hostilities and a political solution. For the North that meant a return of Southern states to the Union with new limitations on the expansion of slavery. For the South the end of the war was imagined as giving birth to a new nation, the Confederate States of America. However, it soon became apparent to both sides that the Civil War would have to play itself out in the same manner as most wars in history: the defeat of armies, the occupation of territory, and, at the end, a single victor.

FEDERAL UNIFORMS

The uniform standards for Federal army, navy, and marine officers and soldiers were detailed in official regulations as to color, style, and trim, but these rules were not always rigorously enforced. By 1863, the varied dress of some volunteer regiments gave way to the regular army uniform: dark blue wool frock or sack coat worn over sky-blue trousers, kepi or forage hat, ankle-high boots, and leather accoutrements. The standardization of sizes in the Civil War allowed mass production of thousands of uniforms.

This did not mean the two sides did not seek alternatives to total war and total victory. At the beginning of hostilities, General Winfield Scott proposed blockading the ports of the South and taking control of the Mississippi River to divide the Confederacy in two. He reasoned that the South would then realize just how much it depended on the North for survival. That did not happen, but elements of Scott's plan formed the foundation for subsequent Northern war strategy. Later in the war, the administration of Abraham Lincoln sought to defeat the South one state at a time by organizing reconstructed governments in conquered territory.

OPPOSITE RIGHT Robert E. Lee as a pre–Civil War U.S. Army officer. He was described as "the best soldier I ever saw in the field" by General Winfield Scott, to whom Lee submitted his resignation.

OPPOSITE LEFT Federal soldiers wearing standard-issue uniforms, which were introduced in 1863.

RIGHT Soldiers dressed in militia uniforms pose before going to war.

BELOW The press derided Winfield Scott's early war plan to strangle the Confederacy with a naval blockade and take control of the Mississippi. However, elements of Scott's plan became part of Federal strategy.

LEFT Northern 90-day volunteers parade in New York City on their way to war.

BELOW Confederate Secretary of War James A. Seddon was the last and most effective in that post, because he acted as support and buffer for President Jefferson Davis.

OPPOSITE ABOVE Supply issues meant that Confederate soldiers were often more haphazardly dressed than their Federal counterparts.

OPPOSITE BELOW In the early morning mist, Union soldiers of the 96th Pennsylvania at Camp Northumberland, near Washington, stage a marching formation with bayonets fixed and arms shouldered.

For its part, the South hoped to force an armistice that would allow it to leave the Union in peace. To do this the Confederates focused their efforts, through diplomacy and battlefield victories, on provoking intervention by the governments of Europe, particularly those of Great Britain and France. General Robert E. Lee's two invasions of the North were undertaken with this goal in mind. At the same time the Confederates hoped to create a sense of "war weariness" on the part of Lincoln's political opponents and the people of the North.

But ultimately, the war was not going to be resolved without the deployment of armies, navies, war command, and matériel. After Fort Sumter was bombarded, President Lincoln put out a call for volunteers to supplement the small number of regulars in the U.S. Army, Navy and Marines. The number of regulars had been diminished by those who left to fight for the South, including such high-ranking officers as Robert E. Lee, who resigned his officer's commission after his native state of Virginia left the Union. The Confederacy also established a small regular army, which mostly performed administrative functions. By the end of the war every state and territory in the Union had provided volunteer regiments or individual soldiers. All eleven seceding states provided volunteer forces to the Confederacy, and the three border states provided troops to both sides.

Tactically and logistically, the Civil War was different from the conflicts that came before it. It was technology that made it the first modern war. The Civil War was the first large-scale conflict in which breech-loading rifles were used. Multishot repeating pistols, carbines, and rifles were all in use. The Napoleonic field tactics of Europe's nineteenth-century wars, in which long lines of infantry faced each other and fired in volleys, were abandoned, as rifled muskets and the new conical minié ball increased the accuracy and impact of infantry weapons. Technology greatly affected naval operations as well. The steam-powered navies featured ironclad ships, pivoting guns, electrically detonated mines, and a host of new vessels, including river rams, torpedo boats, and at least one submarine.

Logistically, the Civil War benefited from the industrial expansion of the era. Not only did industrial technology increase the output and quality of weapons and matériel, industrial inventions also had military uses. Railroads made the largest impact, dramatically improving the mobility of armies and better lines of supply. Samuel F. B. Morse's invention led to adoption of the field telegraph as a command communications tool. Thaddeus Lowe and others developed aerial surveillance using gas balloons. The Confederacy employed commerce

CONFEDERATE UNIFORMS

The Confederacy had its own set of uniform regulations, much of which was adapted from the U.S. Army, but limits on supply required more improvisation in uniform styles. The standard color of Southern army, navy, and marine uniforms was cadet gray, but homespun cloth, often yellow-brown from butternut dye, was also used. As the war dragged on, soldiers in the field had to piece together uniforms, and many new recruits fought in their own clothes, with some regulation insignia, caps, or accoutrements.

raiders on the high seas, while the North used marches through the South aimed at destroying supplies and industry, as ways to affect the logistical capabilities of their enemy.

Finally, although the upper command structure of the armies on both sides incorporated organization by armies, corps, divisions, and brigades, the basic unit of both armies remained the regiment. In the most democratic society in the world at that time, and one in which, at an average age of 23, most soldiers could vote, the structure and command of the forces was conditioned by political as well as military necessity. Volunteer regiments elected their own company officers, and state governors appointed the field officers. Many generals, even those who had been professional soldiers before the war—such as Ulysses S. Grant—received their appointments from state governors. The two opposing administrations were also forced to appoint a large number of men to important commands who had no professional military experience because the constituencies that these political leaders represented were vital to the support of the war effort.

Life in the White House

1861–1865

Abraham Lincoln was a youthful 52 years old when he took the oath of office in 1861. He brought to Washington an ambitious First Lady and three sons: Robert, who was attending Harvard, and Willie and Tad, two young boys with an energy and irreverence unsuited to the stately Executive Mansion.

Soon the pranks of the Lincoln boys became legendary among staff, who bore the brunt of their play. Criticized by Washington's elite as being unrefined Westerners, Mary Todd Lincoln took umbrage at the derogatory comments.

The Executive Mansion, as the White House was officially called throughout Lincoln's administration, had suffered from being neglected under previous administrations. Carpets were worn, draperies faded, tobacco juice stained wallpaper and flooring near spittoons, and furniture was broken or often revealed holes in the upholstery where a souvenir hunter had grabbed a trophy. The key to the front door had been lost years ago, making it impossible to secure the building from intruders.

Mary, therefore, set out to make the Executive Mansion reflect Union strength and beauty. She had a budget of $20,000, but unfortunately Mrs. Lincoln overspent by more than $6,800 and compounded her mistake by trying to hide it from her husband. To cover her indiscretions, she enlisted the help of John Watt, the Executive Mansion gardener, and an adventurer named Henry Wikoff. Watt showed Mary how to double-bill for items: he placed his wife on the government payroll, only to draw her salary for doing no work and give it to Mary Lincoln. Wikoff, meanwhile, had Mrs. Lincoln obtain the president's annual congressional message. Wikoff was on the payroll of the Democratic *New York Herald* that published the remarks in advance of their delivery to Congress. The scandal and government investigation led to the banishment of both Watt and Wikoff from Washington, and congressional Republicans quietly covered the cost overruns.

ABOVE The exterior of the White House, then officially known as the Executive Mansion, as it looked when the Lincolns lived there.

LEFT Tad Lincoln posing as a Union soldier, complete with miniature sword. Tad was a complex child, exuberant and wild. His slightly curious personality may have owed something to a speech impediment that made him all but impossible to understand.

THE SOLDIER DOLL JACK

Willie and Tad Lincoln were often babysat by a girl named Julia Taft, who had two younger brothers about the same age as the Lincoln boys. She remembered them receiving a soldier doll that they named "Jack." They often placed Jack on "guard duty" in outdoor play. The wind frequently knocked Jack over, giving the impression that he was asleep at his post. Such an act was punishable by execution, and the young Lincolns reveled in mock trials and execution. Their habit of burying Jack in the rose garden earned the ire of the Executive Mansion gardener. Appealing to their father to set the gardener straight, Willie and Tad interrupted a presidential meeting. Lincoln listened to his sons' pleas, and rather than oppose the gardener, he wrote out a pardon for the soldier doll, thereby preventing any further such executions.

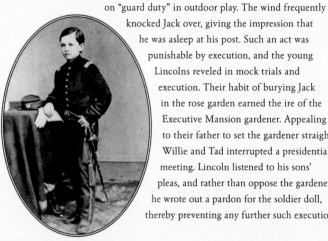

Personal tragedy stuck on February 20, 1862, with the death of Willie Lincoln from typhoid fever at the age of 11. Abraham dealt with his grief by throwing himself into his all-consuming presidential work. With some encouragement from Elizabeth Keckly, Mary's dressmaker, the First Lady turned to spiritualism. Fearing for her husband's health, Mary invited old Illinois friends over for breakfast to force the president to eat. She made him take time away from work for afternoon carriage rides, offering some respite from the misery of the war. The president and First Lady were also frequent visitors to the theater and opera.

Lincoln's average day was long and filled with interruptions. He insisted on getting information directly from sources, not filtered via middlemen, and allowed weekly direct public access on a first-come-first-served basis—a practice he jokingly referred to as his "public opinion baths." In contrast, his meetings with the entire cabinet were infrequent, as he generally dealt with individual members on an as-needed basis.

Southern opposition had prevented previous presidents from inviting blacks to the Executive Mansion. Lincoln, however, allowed delegations of black clergy and notable individuals such as Sojourner Truth and Frederick Douglass to private meetings as well as to public receptions.

ABOVE A ball held at the Executive Mansion, with Lincoln and his wife in the foreground. Lincoln believed that redecorating the Executive Mansion and hosting balls would show the strength and determination of the Union.

RIGHT One of the most famous African Americans to work in Lincoln's administration was William Slade, Lincoln's personal messenger.

Republican Congress

1860–1862

In 1860, the Republican platform became the blueprint for congressional action throughout Lincoln's first term. Following the departure of Southern Democrats during the secession crisis and the firing on Fort Sumter, Republicans lost a sizable opposition and were able to advance their political agenda. Much of it dealt with economic issues such as tariffs and banks—financing the war placed additional burdens on Congress to raise revenues. Other issues concerned infrastructure, such as railroad construction. Distribution of government lands and the creation of schools were instituted to support and strengthen free laborers. The distribution of western lands was to promote free land for free men, an essential element of Republican policies. The policy not only hoped to rapidly settle the vast lands in the territories but it also supported a false hope that the urban poor would leave the cities for the opportunity of a new life as a farmer.

The platform also reaffirmed the rights of immigrants, setting the Republicans apart from the Know-Nothings. The economic planks of the 1860 platform mirrored Lincoln's own views, and he was therefore comfortable deferring to congressional initiatives without executive interference. In fact, Lincoln's political philosophy reflected his Whig origins, which placed

ABOVE An 1864 exterior shot of Washington showing the Capitol Building, the seat of government for the United States Congress, with the now-completed dome.

RIGHT Owen Lovejoy, lawyer, abolitionist, and Republican congressman. He was also a "conductor" on the Underground Railroad and a confidant and loyal supporter of Lincoln's.

Congress in the exclusive role of legislating. Lincoln, however, reserved the right to initiate policy under the constitutional authority of war powers as commander in chief. Decisions regarding the military and emancipation were reserved for the president, not Congress.

The Legal Tender Act, passed on February 26, 1862, authorized Congress to print $150 million in federal currency to cover outstanding debts. Normally, printing money without a subsequent revenue source would lead to inflation, but in July 1862, the Internal Revenue Act was passed and raised $600 million using a graduated income tax. The National Currency Act (1863) created a national banking system and replaced state banking currencies with national banknotes called greenbacks. Treasury bonds were successfully sold by agents such as Jay Cooke, J. Pierpont Morgan, and A. J. Drexel. With Southern opposition removed, tariffs were raised, providing additional sources of revenue to federal coffers.

The Homestead Act (1862) gave any settler who farmed a quarter-section, or 160 acres, for five years a clear title to the property. By 1865, more than 20,000 farmers had acquired land through this legislation.

The Pacific Railroad Act (1862) also advanced the settlement of western lands by constructing a transcontinental railroad to connect the Atlantic and Pacific shores. Before the war, Southerners had pushed for an eastern terminus located somewhere in the South, which lacked a sufficient rail network. Now, however, the Union Pacific began to lay track west from Nebraska and meet the Central Pacific, which was laying track east from California. Finally, the Morrill Act (1862) established the creation and funding of colleges that would promote educational advancements in agriculture and the mechanical arts.

The main achievement of the Republican Congress was the creation of a modern banking and national currency, which was necessary for industrial growth. These economic measures were intended to assist individuals in their quest for personal improvement. Ironically, they also led to the centralization of capital, which brought about the excesses of corporate corruption that followed the war.

FRANK LESLIE'S BUDGET OF FUN

No. 34.   NEW YORK, MARCH 15, 1861.   Price 6 Cents.

GULLIVER ABE, IN THE WHITE HOUSE, ATTACKED BY THE LILLIPUTIAN OFFICE-SEEKERS.

THE CONGRESSIONAL COMMITTEE ON THE CONDUCT OF THE WAR

Created on December 10, 1861, after the Union defeat at Ball's Bluff, Virginia, the Congressional Committee on the Conduct of the War met throughout the conflict to investigate problems. Typically, the committee issued harsh judgments against generals who were not considered aggressive in their war efforts. Lincoln often embraced the committee's findings when they mirrored his own views; both he and the committee agreed that Major General George B. McClellan had not been aggressive enough in his approach, which led to McClellan's dismissal in 1862 after the Battle of Antietam.

ABOVE The comic press shows a new president overwhelmed by office-seekers demanding government jobs.

LEFT Benjamin F. Wade, Ohio radical in the U.S. Senate and chairman of the Congressional Committee on the Conduct of the War.

Fort Donelson to Vicksburg: Grant Strikes

1862–1863

By February 1862, the Union could do no more than contain the Confederate armies. In the east, the Army of the Potomac was still smarting from its humiliations at Bull Run the previous summer. In the strategically critical west, fighting had been sporadic and inconclusive. The Mississippi, the Union's ultimate western goal, seemed not so much elusive as apparently beyond any hope of conquest. So long as it remained in Confederate hands, men and supplies could continue to be funneled north and east from Texas. There seemed no way to break this apparently hopeless stalemate.

The man who would find the way, in the process galvanizing the Union's war efforts, was Ulysses S. Grant. At this stage, he was little more than a largely unknown junior commander whose taste for whiskey was seized on gleefully by his numerous enemies in the Union ranks as clear evidence of unfitness for higher command. He led the 15,000-strong Army of the Tennessee in its capture of the two key

Confederate positions on the Tennessee River, Forts Henry and Donelson, in early February 1862, providing the Union with its first major victory. The death count also made clear to Grant a truth that would color his every subsequent campaign: that this was war that could be won only by the systematic application of force in every sense. There would be no sudden, dazzling victories. The enemy would need to be ground into defeat.

Lincoln at least took the lesson to heart, making clear his support for Grant as the only Union general who had shown any desire for the fight. Grant's immediate superiors on the other hand, McClellan above all, did everything they could to denigrate the new hero of the Union. If their small-minded sniping reflected no credit on them, they could at least claim a degree of vindication when, on April 6, 1862, Grant's Army of the Tennessee, now 40,000 strong and advancing overland against Vicksburg—the remaining key to control of the Mississippi and widely thought impregnable—

ABOVE Major General Ulysses S. Grant scored a major victory at Vicksburg, but it came at a cost. At Vicksburg and beyond, his strategic use of the means of war would be necessary to defeat a determined foe.

LEFT General Joseph E. Johnston had approximately 30,000 soldiers outside Vicksburg who were not engaged in the siege.

OPPOSITE ABOVE Rear Admiral David D. Porter's gunboats take the lead in a run of Federal vessels past the Vicksburg batteries on the night of April 16, 1863. A slow response by the Confederates allowed the flotilla to pass with little damage.

OPPOSITE BELOW LEFT The rifled field gun proved to be a significant weapon during the Civil War.

OPPOSITE BELOW RIGHT The Vicksburg garrison was commanded by Lieutenant General John C. Pemberton. Though a competent soldier, he found himself comprehensively outfought by Grant's Army of the Tennessee.

was overwhelmed by a sudden Confederate attack. Grant appeared routed. The following day, he struck back. The Battle of Shiloh cost 23,000 casualties. It was more than had died in the Revolutionary War, the War of 1812, and the Mexican War combined. Grant's enemies in the Union high command circled again. Meanwhile, the assault on Vicksburg stalled.

It was relaunched only in December. By now a series of riverborne assaults on Vicksburg under Admiral Farragut had been beaten off. A land assault seemed the only answer. Marching his forces south, Grant was then surprised yet again by a Confederate attack behind his lines. His supply base lost, he had no option but to turn north for a second time. The smell of defeat was unmistakable.

Grant's eventual seizure of Vicksburg would prove a model of the attritional warfare he now excelled in. If it depended on the superior resources the Union could bring to bear—in river craft, in guns, in men—it was no less dependent on Grant's willingness and ability to deploy them. On the night of April 16, 1863, he ordered his river transports and gunboats to make a daring descent of the Mississippi past the city. They successfully ran the gauntlet of fire. In the meanwhile, he marched his troops south along the west bank of the river before ordering them across it. By May 16, having successfully repulsed the remaining Confederate forces defending the eastern approaches to Vicksburg, Grant had surrounded the "Gibraltar of the West." He now intended to starve it to death.

The seige lasted 45 days. Vicksburg surrendered on July 4. When the Union forces entered the city, they encountered a population reduced to depths of privation that shocked them all. Grant had not just made the price of victory starkly clear. He had spelled out the reality of defeat.

RIFLED FIELD GUN

Rifled artillery was a development of the 1850s and quickly became a mainstay of Civil War artillery. Smoothbores were useful for short-range purposes and firing a variety of projectiles. The grooves in rifled cannons spun projectiles for long-range accuracy, and exploding shells could be fired up to 2,000 yards. As a result, most batteries had a combination of Napoleons, howitzers, and rifled guns—the three-inch ordnance rifle and the Parrot rifle, in 10- to 30-pounder models, being the most common.

Pemberton, Lieut.-Gen. J. C., of...............Va.

The Naval Struggle

1861–1865

While the war at sea never approached the scale or significance of that on land, it nonetheless played a critical part in the Civil War, not that Lincoln, a landsman first and last, exercised much direct control over it. It was dictated chiefly by the Union's recognition that it was necessary to end the South's access to the sea both to strangle its trade and deny it access to raw materials. Blockading and seizing the near 3,000 miles of Confederate coastline and its numerous ports, large and small, became a key strategic Union goal. Yet it also saw a series of technical innovations, above all in the development of iron warships, that had an immense impact on later naval warfare.

Both sides began the war with modest forces: the North had 40 naval ships, the South in effect none at all. Yet though both made determined efforts to increase these numbers, characteristically it was the North that made the greater progress. For the South, the naval war was a matter of hasty and desperate improvisation.

The early initiative belonged to the North, the capture of Cape Hatteras, North Carolina, in August 1861, followed in November with the seizure of Port Royal, South Carolina, in the first major naval engagement of the war. Yet it was the Confederates who produced the first ironclad, the CSS *Virginia*,

a rapidly converted wooden frigate, the USS *Merrimack*. However lumbering and unmaneuverable, its armor plating rendered it invunerable to attack from wooden ships. The Union responded with the more innovative still USS *Monitor*. The two met memorably on March 9 at Hampton Roads at the mouth of the James River, battering each other at close range for several hours before being forced to retire exhausted. Each claimed the victory.

Clearly, if the wooden warship had been rendered obsolete, the future lay with whichever side could produce the most ironclads. The North's material advantages told decisively. The South was able to produce only one further major ironclad during the rest of the war, built with immense difficulty, the CSS *Tennessee*. The North produced 50, all based on the *Monitor*. The disparity would prove critical.

In April 1862 the North had further success with the capture of New Orleans, easily the largest and most important Confederate port. The assault was part of a two-pronged attack on the Mississippi: south from Kentucky along the river itself, led by a series of heavily armored river gunboats; north from New Orleans. When the two Union forces met at Vicksburg in July 1863, the South had effectively been spilt in two.

LEFT The historic encounter between the ironclads CSS *Virginia*, to the right, and the USS *Monitor* in Hampton Roads on March 8, 1862. To the left is the USS *Cumberland*, engulfed by flames and rapidly sinking after having been rammed by the *Virginia*. The remainder of the wooden Federal fleet remains prudently out of range.

OPPOSITE ABOVE The CSS *H.L. Hunley*, seen here on a Charleston pier in a painting by soldier-artist Conrad Wise Chapman, was an ingenious, though dangerous, submarine. Powered by eight crewmen turning a crank, it was able to ram a torpedo into the stern of the USS *Housatonic* on February 17, 1864, though the vessel and its crew were lost in the sinking ship's wake.

SUBMARINE WARFARE

The sinking of the USS *Housatonic* off Charleston on the night of February 17, 1864, by the CSS *H.L. Hunley* was a notable first. The *Hunley*, however innovative, was far from the first submarine. Vessels more or less capable of operating under the sea had been constructed—and as frequently lost—since the late eighteenth century. But the *Hunley*'s attack on the *Housatonic* was the first time the submarine's potential had been made clear. That said, the *Hunley*, launched the previous July, was almost as dangerous to her eight-man crew as to her intended victims. It had twice sunk during trials, the second time with the loss of all hands. It sank again after the sinking of the *Housatonic*, again taking its crew with it, never to be recovered.

Union forces enjoyed more mixed success in their attempts to seize the remaining Confederate ports. Charleston, South Carolina, stubbornly resisted two major naval assaults, in April and August 1863. In the continuing blockade of the city, the South then enjoyed two notable firsts: the first attack on an ironclad by a torpedo boat, when in October 1863 the CSS *David* severely damaged the USS *New Ironsides*; and the first attack by a submarine on a warship, when in February 1864 the *H.L. Hunley* sank the USS *Housantonic*.

The North's grip tightened inexorably, however. In August 1864 Mobile, Alabama, was taken. It was followed in January 1865 by Wilmington, North Carolina. Charleston fell the next month.

Elsewhere, the naval war was a more patchy affair. It is estimated that perhaps three-quarters of the South's blockade runners—small, swift-sailing ships—evaded capture. But as their business was mostly smuggling luxury goods for the South's dwindling rich, they had little impact on the Confederate ability to prosecute the war. Confederate commerce raiders, by contrast, preying on the North's growing merchant fleet, were a much more persistent menace. In a 21-month cruise, the most celebrated, the CSS *Alabama*, took 60 Northern vessels. Yet here, too, the North prevailed, the *Alabama* eventually battered to destruction in an hour-long action off the coast of northern France by the USS *Kearsage* in June 1864.

ABOVE On August 5, 1864, Rear Admiral David G. Farragut ran his warships past two forts at the mouth of Mobile Bay, but his lead ironclad hit a torpedo (mine) and his column plunged into confusion. Braving the torpedoes, Farragut kept the line of ships moving past the forts and the Confederate squadron, which included the powerful ironclad CSS *Tennessee*.

LEFT Sailors and officers of the USS *Monitor* relax on the steel deck of the ship. The large gun turret is seen in the background. Most Union ironclads were of a design similar to the *Monitor*. The Confederates built ironclads with large casemates similar to the *Virginia*.

The War and Slavery

The preservation of the Union remained Abraham Lincoln's main war objective. In his annual message to Congress on December 3, 1861, Lincoln said that "in considering the policy to be adopted for suppressing the insurrection, I have been anxious that the inevitable conflict for this purpose shall not degenerate into a violent and remorseless revolutionary conflict." The political necessity of maintaining the allegiance of the border states made the discussion of emancipation problematic during the unsettled period of 1861. When General John C. Frémont issued a proclamation that freed the slaves of Missouri rebels on August 30, 1861, this action threatened to undermine the fragile loyalty of Union men in Missouri and Kentucky. Lincoln rescinded Frémont's proclamation at once. In a letter to his friend Orville Browning in 1861, Lincoln argued:

"If the General needs them [slaves], he can seize them, and use them; but when the need is past, it is not for him to fix their permanent future condition. That must be settled according to laws made by law-makers, and not by military proclamations."

LEFT Former slave Frederick Douglass. Following the Emancipation Proclamation (see pages 56–57), Douglass worked with Lincoln to move the newly freed slaves from the South. Douglass also helped to recruit for the 54th Massachusetts Regiment, one of the first official African American units in the U.S. armed forces.

BELOW LEFT An effigy doll reflects the racism of the times. Under Lincoln's face is a black face supporting the charge of "black Republicans."

Lincoln recognized that property could not be confiscated permanently without compensation being given. The continuing problem, however, was how to address the natural rights of individuals who also happened to be defined as constitutionally protected property. On May 9, 1862, General David Hunter attempted to issue a proclamation of emancipation for slaves under his jurisdiction in South Carolina, Georgia, and Florida. Lincoln once again revoked the act, claiming that laws on emancipation were the jurisdiction of the president rather than the military.

Early in the war, General Benjamin F. Butler had cleverly defined slaves as contraband. Northern public opinion supported Butler's creative way of denying Southerners use of their human property, in much the same way as Southerners confiscated Federal property such as forts and garrisons without compensation. As the war progressed, however, retribution for pain and suffering resulted in legislation that was meant to strip the Confederacy of its most prized possession: slaves. The First Confiscation Act was passed on August 6, 1861, which allowed for the confiscation of Confederate property used to support insurrection. Lincoln only reluctantly signed the bill, believing that, ultimately, the courts would overturn its broad mandate. In contrast, he embraced the abolition of slavery in the District of Columbia in a bill passed during April of 1862. Unlike the Confiscation Act, this bill provided compensation to owners for the freedom of their slaves. Lincoln repeatedly tried to offer compensated emancipation to loyalists in the border states, but without success.

Congress then passed an even stronger measure, the Second Confiscation Act, which Lincoln duly signed on July 17, 1862. This act allowed for the freedom of all slaves from areas of the rebellion who crossed into Union territory. Again, although he signed it, the president had grave doubts about the constitutionality of the measure.

The subject of emancipation remained a contentious topic among military generals and soldiers. Many felt that the war was a white man's war only about union. Others, after seeing the horrors of slavery firsthand, became sympathetic to emancipation. Still others saw emancipation as the only practical solution to end the divisive issue.

CONTRABAND

The Constitution protected property rights, and slaves were considered property, not persons; thus fugitive slaves, by law, had to be returned to their masters. When three slaves escaped on May 24, 1861, and ran to freedom at Fortress Monroe, Virginia, commanded by General Benjamin F. Butler, Butler shrewdly declared the fugitive slaves "contraband of war" and thus subject to seizure by Federal forces. The term stuck, because it allowed generals to respect the status of slaves as property while at the same time protecting them from being returned to bondage.

LEFT Fugitive slaves traveling in Virginia in 1862.

BELOW Many people felt frustration at the absence of emancipation as this cartoon from the December 20, 1862, edition of *Harper's Weekly* shows. When it first appeared, the caption below it remarked that emancipation had been postponed until 1900.

The Peninsula to Second Manassas: Lee Triumphant

When Robert E. Lee was given command of the Confederate forces in Virginia–the Army of Northern Virginia, as he styled it–on June 1, 1862, he could hardly have taken over at a more inauspicious moment. Two months earlier, a vast Union army under George B. McClellan, the "Young Napoleon," had landed on the peninsula that stretched to the east of Richmond, the Confederate capital, between the James and York Rivers. It boasted no less than 120,000 men, 15,000 animals, 1,200 wagons, and 44 artillery batteries. It threatened to crush the Confederates, promising the North a swift and emphatic victory. On August 3, it was withdrawn to Washington. McClellan's Army of the Potomac may still have been more or less intact. In every other respect, its "grand campaign" had been an absolute failure.

Yet on Lee's appointment, the leading Union elements had been within five miles of Richmond, so close the Union soldiers could hear church bells in the city. The Confederates had managed an orderly withdrawal to strongly fortified defensive positions in the face of a typically ponderous Union advance. But knowing the city would never be able to withstand a prolonged bombardment, on May 31 the Confederate commander, Joseph E. Johnston, launched an offensive, the Battle of Seven Pines. The fighting was inconclusive. But it took at least some of the sting out of the Union advance. Of much greater significance, however, was what was becoming a depressingly regular feature of the fighting: an alarming casualty rate. And among the casualties was General Johnston. Hence Lee's promotion.

It was the first time the 55-year-old Lee had exercised high command. From the start, he demonstrated something approaching genius in his exercise of it. Acutely conscious that in a purely defensive war, the North's superior resources would wear down the South, he recognized that the Confederacy's best, possibly only, hope of victory was to take the offensive through a series of high-speed campaigns that would leave the enemy bemused and the Northern public, already frustrated by the lack of progress, demoralized. It was inevitably a risky strategy, one dependent, too, on commanders able to carry out Lee's elaborate and complex plans.

He had certain advantages. His army had recently been strengthened and, at 92,000 strong, could now claim near parity with McClellan's Union troops. Likewise, fighting on home soil, the Confederates were not

ABOVE Federal gunboats aid Army of the Potomac units in the Battle of Malvern Hill, July 1, 1862, the last of the Seven Days' battles. Though well-coordinated Union artillery barrages made this a tactical victory, McClellan then withdrew his army from the peninsula.

LEFT This row of 13-inch seacoast mortars was a portion of the armament that Major General George B. McClellan pressed into service for his siege against the thin Confederate line at Yorktown from April 5 to May 3, 1862.

dependent on the long and vulnerable supply lines needed to keep the Union forces in the field, which required 600 tons of supplies a day. And in McClellan, Lee faced an opponent who had consistently shown himself cautious to the point of immobility. "The Great Tortoise," as Lincoln called McClellan, may have been a brilliant military administrator—but he was no fighting general.

Between June 25 and July 1, Lee swept McClellan's Army of the Potomac into a lumbering retreat. The Seven Days' Battle was far from a flawless campaign. On a series of occasions, Union forces were allowed to escape when, with better intelligence and more prompt execution of orders, they might have been overwhelmed. But not only had Richmond been saved, Lee had decisively snatched the initiative from the Union forces. The cost, however, was

predictably high, with 20,000 Confederate casualties to Union losses of 16,000.

In late August, in the Second Battle of Manassas in northern Virginia, Lee inflicted a further crushing defeat on a Union army under Major General John Pope. Dividing his army and then bringing it together in an almost supernatural demonstration of generalship, Lee inflicted a humiliation on Pope that saw the Union man stripped of his command and left to languish in bitter obscurity in Minnesota.

It is hard to overstate the impact of Lee's first three months of command. His victories caused deep dismay in Washington and left Lincoln more distrustful than ever of his generals. However high the cost in men and materials, they simultaneously proved an immense boost to Confederate morale. The new nation looked forward eagerly to further triumphs.

ROBERT E. LEE

Robert Edward Lee (1807–70), son of a hero of the Revolutionary War, graduated with honors from West Point, where he later served as a superintendent. He joined the elite Corps of Engineers and served with distinction under General Winfield Scott in the Mexican War (1846–48). Lee was serving in Texas when the state seceded. With the outbreak of the war, Lincoln and Scott attempted to persuade him to accept command of the Federal forces. This was an offer he refused only after an agony of indecision. But the lure of his native Virginia proved too great for a man to whom loyalty and honor were all. He was a man of immense courtesy and, despite a reserved manner, enormous energy. In the face of significant material disadvantages, he came tantalizingly close to securing an improbable Southern victory against a much stronger foe. Only Grant rivaled him as a commander in the Civil War.

ABOVE LEFT The shattered ruins of the Stone Bridge at Bull Run Creek after Second Manassas.

ABOVE RIGHT Major General George B. McClellan and his wife Marcy. McClellan was from a distinguished Philadelphia family and was successful in every antebellum pursuit: at West Point; in the Mexican War; as an innovative army engineer; and in private business. Civil War historian James McPherson suggests that because he never knew failure, McClellan would not risk it in battle, and consequently never achieved greatness as a military commander.

LEFT A graduate of West Point, under different circumstances Robert E. Lee could have been leader of the Union forces. But, ultimately, he was a loyal Virginian.

Lincoln's Faith

A number of different forms of religious expression comprised Lincoln's ancestry. Samuel Lincoln was a Puritan dissenter, the Pennsylvania Lincolns became Quakers, and his father and stepmother Thomas and Sarah Lincoln were Baptists. Thomas Lincoln served as an elder in the Little Pigeon Creek Baptist Church, where he was called upon to impose church regulations and biblical standards of behavior upon members. Typical infractions included swearing, working on the Sabbath, gossiping, and more serious sins such as adultery. Using his carpentry skills, Thomas built the church and, according to tradition, also utilized the skills of his son Abraham.

It was common for young men not to be church members until after marriage. What set the young Lincoln apart from others was his ability to impersonate people. He is remembered for mocking itinerant ministers by waving his arms wildly and preaching hellfire and brimstone. Later in life Lincoln joked that a minister's sermon is not worth listening to unless he appears as if he is fighting bees. It was at this time that Lincoln received a thorough grounding in the books of the Bible and committed many passages to memory.

Much has been made of Lincoln's flirtation with skepticism in New Salem. He purportedly read the works of a number of deists, including Thomas Paine and Constantin François de Chassebœuf, comte de Volney. That many young adults question the values held by their parents is not unusual, and New Salem was Lincoln's time to experiment with both ideas and careers.

Lincoln was married by Charles Dresser, an Episcopal minister, in a traditional Christian service. The death of their son Eddie (see page 19) led both Abraham and Mary on a faith journey. Mary received comfort from the ministration of James Smith, the minister at the First Presbyterian Church. Smith was an old-school Presbyterian, coming from a tradition in which clergy were required to have formal study before going into the ministry and appealed to reason rather than emotion. This suited Lincoln's temperament because it rejected the emotional and occasionally anti-intellectual tradition he witnessed in his youth. Mary took formal instruction and officially joined the First Presbyterian Church in 1851. This also led to the baptism of their youngest son, Tad. Lincoln did not take formal instruction but enjoyed his conversations with Smith. A number of Lincoln's surviving checks show that he occasionally supported Methodists and Portuguese Presbyterians.

ABOVE The Reverend James Smith of the First Presbyterian Church in Springfield, Illinois.

LEFT The minute book from the Little Pigeon Creek Baptist Church documenting the activities of Thomas Lincoln, a member of the church.

In Washington, the Lincolns typically attended Reverend Gurley's New York Avenue Presbyterian Church, another old-school Presbyterian congregation. There is no evidence that Lincoln ever made a profession of Christian faith, publicly claiming the divinity of Jesus or being baptized. But Lincoln clearly had a deep faith based in biblical teachings. He believed in a supreme power that worked in and through history and that he was part of the unfolding historical events. This accounts for his ability to transcend much of the religious bigotry of the period and to claim "it is quite possible that God's purpose is something different from the purpose of either party." Lincoln never claimed he knew what God's will was, but worked toward goals that he hoped would be pleasing to his Maker. His providential beliefs resonated with the largely Protestant and evangelical American public, who responded favorably to Lincoln's frequent biblical references in his writings and speeches.

THE LINCOLN PEWS

Although Lincoln never joined a church, he frequently attended services. In Springfield, he went to Mary Lincoln's church, the First Presbyterian. The pew the Lincolns rented is on display in the sanctuary. In Washington, D.C., the Lincolns attended St. John's Episcopal Church, where every president since James Madison had visited. The presidential pew is designated within the sanctuary. However, Lincoln more frequently attended the New York Avenue Presbyterian Church, which also has a rental pew that was used by the Lincoln family on public display.

ABOVE The New York Avenue Presbyterian Church, Washington D.C. Lincoln regularly worshipped here during the Civil War and rented a pew for $50 a year.

RIGHT Image of Bishop Matthew Simpson (top) and other Methodist leaders surrounding Lincoln. Lincoln's administration was keen to maintain the support of the Methodists for the Union cause. On May 18, 1864, a delegation from the General Conference of the Methodist Episcopal Church presented Lincoln with a petition of support for the war effort.

Photographed by ED. FLEISCHER & CO., Canton, O.

Antietam, Emancipation, and Fredericksburg

From having been forced to contemplate an exclusively defensive war against the North, Lee's victories in the summer of 1862, aided by Jackson's successes in the Shenandoah Valley, introduced a new element into Confederate strategy: that the issue should be forced and the war taken into the North.

The advantages were obvious. Northern support for the war would be severely shaken if it became clear that the South not only had the means but the will to win. It was already clear that popular opinion in the North was turning against Washington's conduct of the war. The presence of large numbers of Southern troops on Union soil could only shake Northern confidence further. At the same time, a Southern invasion would make the defense of Washington a priority. Troops would have to redeployed to defend it, reducing the numbers in the field. Further, with Lincoln issuing a call for 300,000 extra men, it made sense to strike early, before the new troops were available. There were diplomatic considerations, too. Continuing Southern military success made the prospect of open support from Britain and France, both uneasily neutral to

date, much more likely. If the risks were clear, so too were the potential gains. Thus on September 4, 1862, Lee's men made their fateful move north, crossing the Potomac into Maryland.

Lee's aim was to establish his forces in the east of the state, drawing the Federal forces away from their bases. There, piecemeal, achieving local numerical superiority, he intended to pick them off. Inevitably, reality intruded. Compared to the Union's forces, Lee's troops were underfed, badly equipped, and poorly clothed. Desertions became commonplace. In addition, their welcome in Maryland was ambivalent at best. Slave state or not, Maryland was still part of the Union. The presence of 70,000 invading Confederates, demanding food and shelter and able to pay only with devalued Confederate dollars, provoked predictable resentment. Worst of all, having yet again split his forces, Lee's orders for their subsequent deployment were discovered by Federal troops and promptly handed to McClellan, retained in command by Lincoln not because the president had faith in him but because there was no credible alternative.

Even now, McClellan was unable to take advantage of this spectacular Confederate blunder. When the armies met on September 17, the Confederates dug in behind Antietam Creek outside the town of Sharpsburg, McClellan

displayed his usual indecisiveness. Though precisely forewarned of Lee's intentions and with significant reserves of fresh troops, McClellan pursued his attack halfheartedly at best. Hugely outnumbered and outgunned, Lee nonetheless managed an orderly withdrawal. Yet the costs had been devastating: 3,654 men died in one day. It remains the single bloodiest day in American history.

If it was no victory for the North, whatever McClellan's bombast to the contrary, it at least put a temporary stop to the South's hopes of victory in the North. It also provided Lincoln with sufficient breathing space to issue his preliminary Emancipation Proclamation, declaring that on January 1, 1863, all Southern slaves would be freed. However bold an assertion, it could necessarily have little practical effect on the ground. But it made plain that just as Lee had dramatically gambled the South's future, first in the peninsula, now in Maryland, Lincoln, whatever the political and military pressures he faced, was ready to put in place a similarly bold escalation of the North's war aims.

There was one further, bitter coda to come. On November 7, goaded beyond endurance by McClellan's continued, high-handed vacillations, Lincoln sacked him. On December 13, 1862, his replacement, Major General Ambrose E. Burnside, desperate to deliver a Union victory, initiated perhaps the most pointless and brutal slaughter of the entire war at Fredericksburg in northern Virginia. In bitter weather and against deeply entrenched Confederate troops, he sent wave after wave of men to their deaths before being forced to withdraw. In North and South alike, confronting what appeared an unwinnable war, a kind of despair was descending.

JAMES LONGSTREET

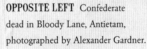

Longstreet was one of Lee's most reliable and trusted commanders. He attended West Point with Grant and Sherman before serving in the Mexican War, where he was wounded. Though the Georgian sought an administrative role in the Confederacy, he was given a field command, and, other than after his wounding at the Battle of the Wilderness in the summer of 1864, served with the Confederates from First Manassas to Appomattox. Though Lee called him "my old warhorse," Longstreet could be slow to follow orders, noticeably on the second day of the Battle of Gettysburg. But he fought unfailingly fiercely when combat began.

OPPOSITE LEFT Confederate dead in Bloody Lane, Antietam, photographed by Alexander Gardner.

OPPOSITE RIGHT Federal infantry advance toward Dunker Church, the location of rebel artillery at Antietam and an objective of the early morning fighting that raged in a cornfield, surrounded by woods on three sides.

ABOVE, TOP General Lee's "old warhorse," James Longstreet.

ABOVE Major General Ambrose E. Burnside did not feel qualified to lead the Army of the Potomac in late 1862. It is said Burnside only took the job to prevent his rival, Major General Joseph Hooker, from getting it.

LEFT Lincoln and his cabinet, to whom he read, to their considerable surprise, his preliminary Emancipation Proclamation in the immediate aftermath of the Battle of Antietam. It was published on September 22, 1862.

Chancellorsville

Despite its string of failures to take Richmond in 1861 and 1862, by the spring of 1863 the Union was poised to mount a further, even larger campaign against Virginia. Its overwhelming superiority in men and matériel was such that it was confidently believed in Washington that this time even the genius of Lee would prove inadequate. Richmond would surely fall, the war as surely be brought to an end.

The optimism stemmed in part from the appointment in January 1863 of a new commander of the Army of the Potomac, Major General "Fighting" Joseph Hooker. Hooker instituted a thorough overhaul of his command, reinforcing his reputation not just as an aggressive commander but as a tough-minded military administrator. Morale was distinctly raised.

On April 30, Hooker ordered his army, almost 135,000 strong, over the Rappahannock River toward the town of Chancellorsville. Confronting them was a disbursed Confederate force under Lee of slightly more than 60,000 men. Hooker's plan was sound: to envelop the Confederate position from the left and right while simultaneously dispatching a large cavalry unit south behind the Confederate army to cut its supply lines.

It failed, in the process giving Lee what is widely claimed his most brilliant victory. However well conceived his tactics, Hooker, by turns blustering and timid, proved startlingly inept in executing them, consistently unable to adapt to changing circumstances and seemingly constitutionally incapable of risk. He also failed to appreciate the nature of much of the terrain over which he was fighting, particularly the tangled ground, the aptly named Wilderness, that surrounded much of Chancellorsville. This not merely disguised the movements of the Confederates, it nullified the firepower of the Union troops. But overwhelmingly his failure was the result of a series of brilliantly daring and unexpected moves by Lee to which, in the end, Hooker had no answer.

The bulk of the battle was fought over three days, from May 1 to 3. On the first, Lee, while leaving a small force of 10,000 to hold off Hooker's attack on his right flank at Fredericksburg, concentrated on hemming the bulk of the Union attack within the Wilderness. That night, he and his most famous commander, the dashing "Stonewall" Jackson, conceived a remarkable ruse. Jackson was to lead 30,000 men on a grueling 12-mile march to the west of the Union forces before bursting upon them from the rear. As at Second Manassas, Lee was disregarding the most basic of military tenets: concentration of your forces against the main enemy. As Jackson led his men north, unbeknownst to Hooker the vast bulk of his army was now facing little more than a near token force of 15,000 men.

Late in the afternoon of May 2, Jackson's troops smashed into the stunned Union flank, scattering it. For the Confederates, it was a moment of vindication marred only by the wounding of Jackson, shot by his own snipers. Eight days later he died. "I do not know how to replace him," said Lee.

If Jackson's attack was plainly the decisive moment of the battle, even now the odds still strongly favored Hooker. Yet put simply, he lost his nerve. May 3 saw wave after wave of Confederate attacks, in the face of which Hooker progressively withdrew his forces. By May 4, a brief Federal rally west of Fredericksburg had been snuffed out. The following day, a somber Hooker

ordered his troops back across the Rappahannock. On June 28, Hooker petutantly offered to resign. Lincoln accepted his resignation with alacrity. Like his predecessor, Burnside, he had lasted just one battle.

Chancellorsville may have been yet another Lee triumph in the face of overwhelming odds, but the battle continued a grim Civil War pattern. As set-piece battle followed set-piece battle, each saw heavier casualties. At Chancellorsville, overall Union losses were 1,600 dead, 10,000 wounded, and 6,000 captured; Confederate losses 1,700 dead, 9,000 wounded, and 2,000 captured.

J.E.B. STUART

Virginian James Ewell Brown Stuart was under 30 when he assumed command of Lee's cavalry corps in the summer of 1862. As West Point superintendent, Lee knew Cadet Stuart and later called upon him to help put down John Brown's uprising at Harpers Ferry. Stuart, known for his resplendent dress, fine horsemanship, and gentlemanly manner, led his well-trained troops ably in reconnaisssance and in combat from First Manassas to his death at Yellow Tavern in May 1864. He was a commander respected by Southerners and Northerners alike.

OPPOSITE LEFT A period lithograph portrays how the last meeting of Robert E. Lee and his most trusted subordinate Thomas "Stonewall" Jackson might have looked prior to Jackson leaving for his flanking march at Chancellorsville.

OPPOSITE RIGHT Confederate dead at the stone wall in Fredericksburg after the assault by the Federal VI Corps in the Battle of Chancellorsville. The same stone wall that had been such an ally in the Battle of Fredericksburg proved to be vulnerable when held by Jubal Early's thin ranks on May 3, 1863.

ABOVE LEFT An artist's impression of a Confederate attack on Major General Hooker's headquarters at Chancellorsville.

ABOVE RIGHT Major General Joseph Hooker was an officer known for personal bravery, but also for intrigue. He proved to be a capable subordinate, but good judgment gave way to caution and uncertainty when he was given overall command.

LEFT James Ewell Brown Stuart, "Jeb" to his friends, was a trusted member of General Lee's Confederate army.

Gettysburg: Punishment and Redemption

Just as the Union in 1863 had been determined to attempt another assault on Virginia, so, following the Confederate triumph at Chancellorsville, Lee and Jefferson Davis were determined to relaunch the Southern invasion of the North, which the stalemate at Antietam the previous year had forced them to abandon. Their reasons remained the same: the South could never win a purely defensive war; the enemy needed to be confronted.

But Lee was conscious, too, that the more military pressure brought to bear on the North, the more the Democrats in the Union would be strengthened. The repeated failure of Union arms had already left Lincoln under intense political pressure. With a presidential election the following year, further Southern success would make a Democrat victory all the more likely. It was almost certain that a new Democrat administration in Washington would seek an immediate settlement to the war. It was no less certain that any such settlement would mean the retention of slavery in the South. It was Lincoln's nightmare.

GEORGE G. MEADE

Major General George G. Meade was the son of an agent for the U.S. Navy. The military was not his first career choice. However, after attending West Point and serving in the Mexican War, he became a noted U.S. Army engineer. Before Gettysburg, he served with distinction in all the major campaigns of the Army of the Potomac, calamitous though they mostly were. Lincoln appointed him its commander, a post he accepted with reluctance, only three days before the Battle of Gettysburg began. He remained in command of the Army of the Potomac until the end of the war, though from March 1864 Ulysses S. Grant was the commanding general of all Union armies.

BELOW A Federal cannon is moved from its position on Cemetery Hill as two brigades of Confederates attack.

ABOVE Major General George G. Meade led the Federal forces to victory over Lee's Confederate army at Gettysburg, despite only taking command three days before the battle.

So from early June, Lee's troops began the march from Virginia into Maryland and from there to Pennsylvania. It was part of Lee's distinctive style of command that he preferred never to tie himself to a definite tactical plan, aiming instead to exploit opportunities as and when they presented themselves, counting on the superior fighting spirit of his men as well as the elastic structure of command and control that had served him so well.

As ever, the risks were clear. And it was on the march northward that the flaws began to show. As the Confederates were unable to carry sufficient supplies to feed themselves, they were forced to forage, living off the land. Yet not only were they now confronted with a deeply hostile population (whom they inevitably brutalized: pillaging, looting, and raping despite Lee's earnest entreaties that his men behave "with most scrupulous care"); to make the most of their scavenging the troops had to be widely dispersed, advancing on a broad, thin front. Communicating with such scattered forces posed immediate difficulties.

There were other difficulties. With few reliable maps, Lee had little information about the nature of the terrain he was approaching. More worrying by far, Lee had almost no information as to the whereabouts of the Army of the Potomac. He knew it must be shadowing the Confederates to their right, keeping itself between Lee and Washington. But where precisely it was, he had no real idea.

It was a problem compounded by an apparent misunderstanding between Lee and his charismatic cavalry commander, Jeb Stuart. For Lee, Stuart's most important role was to update him on the progress of the Union forces. Stuart, on the other hand, though aware of the need to screen Lee, assumed that this was a task that could wait. For now, harassing the enemy would be his prime goal. And thus he disappeared to the east, effectively depriving the Army of Northern Virginia of its prime source of intelligence as well as one its most experienced commanders.

ABOVE LEFT A dead Confederate sharpshooter in Devil's Den. The large natural formation of granite boulders shielded the Confederates, who used the location to snipe on Union soldiers on Little Round Top.

ABOVE RIGHT In the 1880s, the Chicago firm of Kurz & Allison produced a series of vivid lithographs depicting scenes from the Civil War, such as their imagined image of the Battle of Gettysburg. The pictures aimed to evoke the spirit of the conflict rather than to re-create its historical accuracy. Unsurprisingly, they proved very much more popular among Union veterans than their Confederate counterparts.

LEFT Lieutenant Bayard Wilkeson directs Federal artillery north of Gettysburg on July 1. Wounded, he coolly amputated his partially severed right leg with a pocketknife. Hours later he died, bringing anguish to his father, Samuel Wilkeson, a *New York Times* reporter covering the battle.

By June 29, Lee was alarmed to learn that the Union army had closed to within miles. On June 30, an advance unit of Federal cavalry entered Gettysburg, only eight miles from where Lee was now attempting to reassemble his main army at the equally obscure town of Chambersburg. The same day, a small force of Confederate infantry entered Gettysburg. Meeting the Federal troops, it hastily withdrew.

Lee had never intended to fight at Gettysburg. The first he knew of the fighting there was not until almost noon the following day, July 1, when a much larger force of Confederate infantry engaged the Union cavalry in the town. By mid-afternoon, what had begun as a skirmish had dramatically escalated, as more and more troops were drawn into the fighting. From the most unlikely of beginnings, Lee found himself in a major battle he had neither expected nor prepared for. Almost from the start, it became a matter of scrambled improvisation.

At the time, no one suspected that the subsequent fighting, which lasted until late on the afternoon of July 3, would prove the decisive encounter of the Civil War, as well as perhaps its most poignant. When it was over, no one could deny that the Confederates under Lee had been defeated for the first time. But the Confederate army was able to retire in more or less reasonable order, the Union forces, to Lincoln's despair, too exhausted to mount an

effective pursuit. When the news was received of Grant's near simultaneous triumph at Vicksburg, it seemed a vastly more significant victory.

Yet perhaps the most obvious lesson of Gettysburg was that Lee's fabled luck seemed at last to have deserted him. On the second day of the battle, he planned a major assault on the heights to the south of the town, where the Union troops had established themselves en masse. Uncertain of the topography and ignorant of the strength of the Union forces, he was then bedeviled by a series of blunders. Troops were maneuvered with painful slowness, orders lost, misunderstood, or ignored. Even so, as the fighting, rarely less than bitter, developed on both flanks of the Union positions, the Confederates came tantalizingly close to a decisive breakthrough.

Day three, July 3, offered similar glimpses of glory. In what amounted to a final throw of the dice, Lee ordered a frontal assault on the Union's central position. This, Pickett's Charge, was simultaneously a magnificently defiant assertion of Confederate military prowess and a disturbing foretaste of greater slaughters to come. Of the 12,500 men who went forward, two out of every three failed to return to the rebel lines. In three days, 7,058 men had been killed. It may not yet have been immediately obvious, but for Lee and the Confederates the tide had turned. The great gamble had failed on the killing fields of the North.

The Gettysburg Address

The Gettysburg Address was delivered by Lincoln at the dedication of the Soldiers' National Cemetery on the site of the battlefield on November 19, 1863, on a still, sultry afternoon. Though only ten sentences and 270 words long (268 in a rival version), its economy adding to its impact, it constitutes his most eloquent justification for the terrible war now unfolding.

In 1861, Lincoln had described the American Revolution as "a great promise to the world." In a world dominated by various forms of authoritarian rule, the United States was the sole representative of democracy. Preserving it, whatever the hideous cost, was a moral imperative that could not be ducked.

Yet Lincoln's address did not merely look backward to the birth of the United States. It looked forward to what he called "a new birth of freedom." And by this he meant that the Civil War represented a kind of "unfinished work." The new nation had been "conceived in liberty" yet it denied liberty to four million slaves. The Declaration of Independence, to which Lincoln specifically referred in the address, had asserted that "all men are created equal." The Constitution, on the other hand, had defined liberty rather differently, specifically the liberty to own slaves.

This the Gettysburg Address directly confronted with its final, ringing endorsement: "that government of the people, by the people, for the people shall not perish from the earth." This was Lincoln's "unfinished work."

The speech had another purpose, too: to make sense of the appalling loss of life. There can be little doubt Lincoln was profoundly shocked that the war he pursued with such vigor had seen such enormous casualties and, at the time of the address, seemed certain to see further such carnage. Tellingly, in speaking of "these honored dead," he makes no distinction between those of the North and those of the South. The sacrifices of all are equally worthy of respect. All gave "the last full measure of devotion."

EDWARD EVERETT AT GETTYSBURG

In his Gettysburg Address, Lincoln claimed that "the world will little note, nor long remember what we say here." It was one of the few occasions when, at least with reference to his own speech, he was unequivocally wrong. But he could hardly have been more prescient when it came to what had been intended would be the centerpiece of the dedication: an address by the most celebrated orator of the day, the immensely distinguished and now very elderly Edward Everett, politician, linguist, and educator. His speech, 13,607 words long, took over two hours to deliver. Only when this mammoth peroration was completed did Lincoln rise to speak. Everett later wrote to the president: "I should be glad if I could flatter myself that I came as near to the central idea of the occasion, in two hours, as you did in two minutes."

ABOVE Edward Everett was the featured orator at the dedication ceremony of the Gettysburg National Cemetry in 1863.

LEFT An artist's impression of Abraham Lincoln's now famous Gettysburg Address, in which the president examined the founding principles of the United States (the Declaration of Independence) in the context of the Civil War. The only known photograph of Lincoln at Gettysburg was taken several hours before his speech.

The United States Colored Troops

However urgent the need for manpower in the Civil War, at least at the start of hostilities both North and South, the latter above all, were extremely reluctant to recruit blacks into their respective military forces. This may have been understandable in the South, where the last thing the Confederacy wanted were groups of armed blacks potentially rising up against their former masters. The point was precisely demonstrated by the attitude adopted toward the Louisiana Native Guards, which was formed in New Orleans in May 1861 and consisted of free blacks, most French-speaking Creoles. Before its hasty disbanding a year later, it was consistently sidelined by the Confederates, who refused even to clothe let alone arm it. (Of its 1,100 men, about 10 percent subsequently served with the Union army.) It wasn't until March 1865, with the war effectively lost, that the Confederate Congress finally agreed to recruit blacks; even then, they managed to enlist less than 50.

Prejudices in the North toward black troops may have been less entrenched but were real enough despite the potential for recruitment offered by a free black population approaching 400,000. As in the South, it was generally felt that blacks were inherently unsuited for military service, lacking both discipline and fighting spirit, this despite the fighting record of black troops in the past. For Lincoln at any rate there was also a political dimension to consider: the creation of black military units risked alienating opinion in the five slave-owning border states in the Union. It was a problem already made acute in August 1861 when Congress passed the First Confiscation Act, which allowed for all captured Confederate property, including slaves, to be confiscated by the Union. A Second Confiscation Act in July 1862 clarified that any such confiscated slaves would be freed and so in theory at least eligible for armed service.

COME AND JOIN US BROTHERS.

In reality there can be little doubt that Lincoln tacitly supported both measures, despite his public opposition to them, a point highlighted by his Emancipation Proclamation of January 1863, which declared all slaves to have been freed. However hesitantly, the recruitment of black soldiers followed at once, with the United States Colored Troops (USCT) formally established in May 1863.

By the end of the war, its 178,000 men, divided into 175 units, comprised fully 10 percent of the Union army and fought in all theaters of the war, serving as infantry, cavalry, and artillery. By January 1865, USCT numbers alone were greater than those in the entire Confederate army. Yet prejudices remained. Most obviously, all USCT units were never integrated with white units (all U.S. troops were segregated on color lines until 1948). In much the same way, black units were disproportionately assigned menial tasks behind the lines, particularly heavy laboring. For the first year of the USCT's existence, its soldiers were also paid less than their white counterparts, $10 a month as opposed to $16. As tellingly, all the USCT officers were white.

Yet even if their opportunities were limited, USCT men distinguished themselves on numerous occasions, most notably during the bitter fighting at Fort Wagner in July 1863, as Union forces struggled to capture Charleston; at Petersburg in July 1864, the so-called Battle of the Crater, suffering very heavy losses; and the successful storming of Fort Harrison in Virginia in September 1864. In all, 15 members of the USCT were awarded the Medal of Honor, the nation's highest military award, during the war.

WILLIAM H. CARNEY

As a member of the 54th Massachusetts Regiment, Sargeant William. H. Carney served as a color bearer. The July 18, 1863, attack on Fort Morris in Charleston Harbor by the 54th resulted in 281 casualties for the regiment. Carney was the first African American to receive the Medal of Honor from the U.S. Army for recovering the Federal colors in the hand-to-hand struggle. After the battle, he proudly described his actions: "The old flag never touched the ground, boys."

In general, the soldiers of the USCT suffered substantially higher losses than white soldiers: 20 percent of the African American forces lost their lives, a total of 36,000 men. The proportion of those succumbing to disease rather than being killed in action was more in line with troops elsewhere, approximately two-thirds to one-third. Yet USCT men faced a hazard other Union forces never had to contend with: those captured by Confederate troops were frequently murdered out of hand as insurgents rather then being held prisoner or exchanged.

OPPOSITE ABOVE A recruitment poster encourages ex-slaves and free African Americans to join in the defense of the Union.

OPPOSITE BELOW The band of the 107th USCT at Fort Corcoran, Arlington, Virginia. The brass instruments held by the musicians—cornets and saxhorns—were the mainstays of the military brass band.

ABOVE RIGHT William. H. Carney, noted for his heroics at Fort Morris in July 1863.

RIGHT The Battle of the Crater in a sketch by Alfred R. Waud. The gallery under the portion of the rebel line held by the 19th and 22nd South Carolina has just exploded in the background. That signaled the start of Federal artillery fire as a prelude to the infantry assault.

The Civil War Home Front

1861–1865

To many, the war was seen as a great patriotic effort. Stationery and envelopes were illustrated with the Union shield, images of President Lincoln, and generals who distinguished themselves in battle. There was no censorship of soldier or civilian mail. The war was personalized in that husbands or sons on the front lines sent vivid descriptions of battles and what they saw in the South back home.

Of American military conflicts, none has a more extensive and vivid literary documentation than the Civil War letters and diaries between soldiers and their families. Illustrated newspapers and periodicals such as *Frank Leslie's* and *Harper's* presented woodcuts of battles, politicians, and generals who defined the conflict. Lithographers and printmakers provided images of

the war, usually bloodless and stylized, that were purchased by middle-class patrons. Popular music supported the war with memorable tunes such as "Dixie," "The Battle Cry of Freedom," and "When Johnny Comes Marching Home." Photographer Mathew Brady provided the most graphic images of the aftermath of battle with scenes of dead soldiers.

War demands dramatically affected industrial output and, in some instances, urbanization. Chicago's meatpacking industry received large government contracts to provide meat to Union forces, tripling the industry's size in just the first two years. Northern agriculture had a similar boost in production to meet the demands of war. Technological innovations such as the McCormick reaper allowed farmers to expand production with fewer

LEFT The Civil War had an impact on all aspects of life—board games such as this one entitled Running the Blockade were popular with children during the war. The object of the game was to run between the lines of the blockading squadron and reach Wilmington, North Carolina.

OPPOSITE ABOVE LEFT A poster advertising the 1864 Sanitary Fair in New York. In order to raise money for the U.S. Sanitary Commission, Sanitary Fairs were held. The 1864 New York Sanitary Fair featured dances, parades, the sale of merchandise, a cattle show, and an auction. It raised over two million dollars for medical care.

OPPOSITE ABOVE RIGHT A scene of Thirty-second Street showing a Negro having been hung by a mob while houses burn, from the final day of the New York draft riots.

OPPOSITE BELOW Clement Laird Vallandigham, one of the most famous copperheads during the Civil War and generally recognized as their leader. Although he personally objected to slavery, he was a staunch believer in states' rights, felt the Confederacy had the right to secede, and did not believe the Federal government had the power to regulate slavery.

laborers. Factories that produced weapons, uniforms, and other materials for a war economy flourished. Workers and laborers found employment and an increase in their wages that was aided by war inflation. Government policies that expanded railroad construction and consolidated financial institutions set the foundation for the industrial revolution that would follow the war, but also contributed to the decline of state banks and local production of goods. Yet the war also produced a generation of veterans with disabilities. The United States Sanitary Commission offered women many opportunities for work and service. Volunteers not only served as nurses but many became active in fund-raising, administration, and assisting returning veterans. Organizational and leadership skills acquired during the war were used in the years following it to campaign for women's rights.

As the horrors of battle became visible in the North, volunteers who had overwhelmed the state militia rolls sharply declined. Federal conscription was passed on March 3, 1863, to fill necessary Union manpower needs. Bounties, or monetary bonuses, were offered by some states as an incentive. Opposition to the draft often led young men to hide from enrollment officers; occasionally, violence broke out and officers were shot. In New York City, a full-scale riot occurred from July 13 to 15, 1863, as working-class mobs burned, looted, and terrorized the streets. Specifically targeting blacks because they believed that the conflict had become a war to free slaves, rioters burned a black orphanage. At the end of the rampage, about 117 people were dead.

The blockade of Southern ports began to have consequences midway into the war. As more food and clothing were directed to the military, it became increasingly more difficult to provide these items to civilians. Food and materials shortages were exacerbated by merchants hoarding items and selling them for higher prices on the black market. In April 1863, a group of 300 Richmond, Virginia, working-class women protested about the food shortage. Upset by the lack of concern by officials, the women began looting bakeries and other stores, taking bread and meat for their families. Similar riots occurred throughout the South. Shortages caused by the war brought into sharp focus the tensions between the wealthy and the working classes.

COPPERHEADS

As the war progressed, early demonstrations of bipartisanship began to break down as anti-war Democrats openly criticized Lincoln's policies of suspending civil liberties and emancipation. Republicans responded by labeling their critics "copperheads," a reference to a poisonous snake that hid in tall grass and attacked without warning. Soon, many Republicans were using the term to apply to all Democrats, not just the anti-war ones.

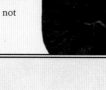

The Butcher's Bill

O ne of the most striking features of the Civil War was that while it may have been the first industrial war, one fought with modern, mass-produced weapons of immense destructive power, advances in battlefield medicine and treatment were much slower to develop. The inevitable result was not just the largest death toll of any American war, but the creation of a series of new armies—of the permanently, often hideously, maimed.

Certainly, on the Union side especially, almost always more lavishly equipped than the Confederates, there were striking improvements in medical provision as the war progressed, above all in the numbers of ambulances and field hospitals, later of permanent hospitals behind the lines. Nursing, too, was transformed, with for the first time women very much to the fore (there were 20,000 Union nurses by the end of the war). As important was the growth in the numbers of doctors. At the start of the war, the Union had 98 army doctors (or surgeons), the Confederacy 24. By the end of the war, the numbers were respectively 10,000 and 4,000. The organization of military medicine was similarly overhauled, again with the North taking the lead, especially after the appointment as Surgeon General in 1862 of Brigadier General William A. Hammond, who effected a dramatic and lasting reconstruction of military medical care. Similar efforts by the medical director of the Army of the Potomac, Jonathan Letterman, produced a service efficient enough to have removed all the Union wounded from the battlefield at Gettysburg the day they fell.

Civilian efforts contributed. The establishment in 1861 of the privately organized, though federally backed, U.S. Sanitary Commission provoked fund-raising efforts across the North in the form of Sanitary Fairs, notably in Chicago, Cincinnati, Baltimore, and Boston. The most impressive, styling itself the Great Central Fair and visited by Lincoln himself, was held in Philadelphia in June 1864. It raised over $1 million for the medical care of Union soldiers.

Yet whatever these advances, the numbers of the dead and wounded remain sobering. The real killer was disease, brought about by alternating combinations of filth, heat, cold, and a nearly nonexistent understanding of the dangers of infections. Excluding the war's 50,000 civilian dead, the generally accepted figure for total Civil War deaths is 620,000: 360,000 Union, 260,000 Confederate. Yet of these, two-thirds were victims of disease. Typhoid, dysentery, and pneumonia accounted for most; chicken pox and measles for many of the rest. Malaria was a similarly persistent problem, with an estimated 25 percent of all combatants falling victim to it: there were a reported one million cases in the Union forces alone. The ready availability of quinine meant that this at least could generally be successfully treated.

The prospects for those wounded in battle were discouraging. Partly because of the sheer numbers of the wounded, partly because of the advent of improved artillery, particularly high-explosive and canister shells, and the development of the minié ball—which expanded on impact, destroying tissues and shattering bones—the best many could hope for was amputation. A contemporary account paints the picture in stark terms:

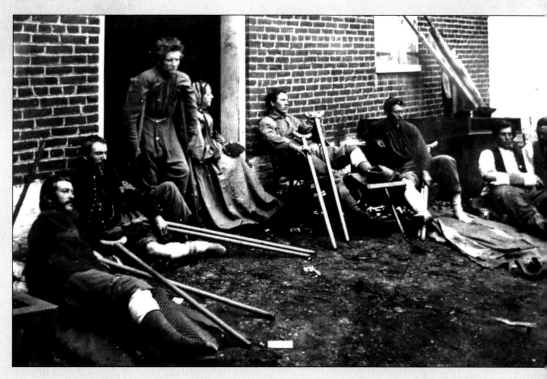

Tables about breast high had been erected upon which the screaming victims were having legs and arms cut off. The surgeons and their assistants, stripped to the waist and bespattered with blood, stood around, some holding the poor fellows while others, armed with long, bloody knives and saws, cut and sawed away with frightful rapidity, throwing the mangled limbs on a pile nearby as soon removed.

Most estimates suggest that about 80,000 such amputations were carried out during the war, each taking an average of 12 minutes. Whatever the horrors, anesthetics of a kind were mostly available, chiefly chloroform. In its absence, whiskey could always be used (1,000 gallons of it at Gettysburg). Morphine, liberally dispensed, was the most common painkiller. Surprisingly or not, 75 percent such amputees survived. After the war, it was calculated that one out of every 13 veterans had lost limbs.

LEFT The polished steel saw for amputating shattered limbs was a part of every surgeon's kit.

CLARA HARLOWE BARTON

Precisely as Florence Nightingale, through sheer force of personality, had transformed Britain's hitherto negligible treatment of its war wounded in the Crimean War (1853–56), so Clara Barton effected similarly sweeping changes in the care of the North's wounded. From the very start of the conflict, she organized relief programs and launched fund-raising drives to provide medical supplies. She was no less active in the field, traveling to many battlefields as well as initiating a program to track missing soldiers and to notify their families. In 1881, she founded the American Red Cross.

OPPOSITE ABOVE The grim reality of war. A Federal surgeon prepares an amputation as others look on.

OPPOSITE BELOW A line of Federal ambulances parked without their teams, waiting to go into action. These vehicles greatly aided in the recovery of wounded soldiers by quickly and safely removing them from the field of battle.

ABOVE Federal soldiers convalesce in a ward at Armory Square Hospital, Washington, D.C.

LEFT Clara Harlowe Barton, founder of the American Red Cross.

Total War: Sherman and Atlanta

Lincoln's appointment in March 1864 of General Grant as commander of all Union forces launched the Civil War on its long, final, brutal phase. As Grant had made clear at Vicksburg in the summer of 1863 and then at Chattanooga, Tennessee, later that year, victory would be achieved only by a grimly attritional struggle in which the superior resources of the Union in men and matériel were deployed relentlessly. "I can't spare this man," Lincoln had said of Grant after the near disaster of Shiloh. "He fights."

In May 1864, for the fourth time in as many years, Federal forces invaded Virginia to be confronted, again, by Lee's Army of Northern Virginia. At almost exactly the same moment, William Tecumseh Sherman, who had fought with Grant in the Vicksburg and Chattanooga campaigns and had since been made commander of the Union forces in the west, launched a massive campaign against Joseph E. Johnston's Confederate Army of Tennessee.

Grant, in Virginia, directed both operations. His goal was simple: to exert the maximum pressure on the Confederacy in the maximum number of different theaters.

Sherman and Grant, the one gruffly outspoken, the other taciturn, neither remotely comparable to the Union army's previous commanders, whose high-minded declarations of imminent victory had invariably ended in defeat, had much in common. As Sherman put it: "Grant stood by me when I was crazy, and I stood by him when he was drunk, and now we stand by each other." They formed a remarkable pairing.

WAR IS HELL

"I am tired and sick of war. Its glory is all moonshine. It is only those who have neither fired a shot nor heard the shrieks and groans of the wounded who cry aloud for blood, for vengeance, for desolation. War is hell." Sherman's most famous quotation precisely encapsulates the paradox of this reluctant but supremely effective warrior, after Grant by some measure the North's most successful general. The recognition that war had now abandoned even the most superficial claims to honor or gallantry to become instead a means of exterminating the enemy in the largest possible numbers in the most efficient possible way was chilling enough. That civilians were now to be numbered among the targets was vastly more disturbing. It is to Sherman's lasting credit that his readiness to acknowledge the necessity of such means was matched by his revulsion for it.

Sherman, with an average of 100,000 troops against Johnston's 60,000, intended to advance south along the line of the Western & Atlantic Railroad toward Atlanta, Georgia, a critical Confederate depot from which supplies were fed to all the Confederate forces in Tennessee and Georgia. Its fall would deal a crippling blow to the Confederate war effort in the Deep South.

Knowing that the Confederates had established a series of strongly defended positions along the line of the railroad, in exactly the same way that Atlanta, too, was now shielded by a 10-mile ring of defenses, Sherman determined to outflank the Confederate defenses wherever possible, risking frontal assaults only as a last resort. Confronted by this inexorable Union advance, Johnston found himself obliged to order a series of withdrawals. However much sense they made tactically, they provoked mounting dissatisfaction in the Confederate leadership. Even the one major Union defeat in the campaign, when an attack on the strongly entrenched Confederate positions on Kennesaw Mountain at the end of June was bloodily repulsed, proved insufficient to save Johnston. On July 17, with Sherman having by now outflanked the Confederate defenses and within striking distance of the city, Johnston was sacked.

His replacement, John Bell Hood, immediately launched a series of more or less desperate assaults on Sherman's forces. Whatever minor, local successes Hood enjoyed, they could do nothing to alter the fact that Sherman's army now surrounded Atlanta. Besieged, its capitulation was a matter of time. On September 2, the city surrendered. Sherman sent a laconic telegram to Lincoln: "Atlanta is ours, and fairly won."

In important ways, Sherman's capture of Atlanta only hinted at the destruction a modern army single-mindedly led could cause. By mid-November, having decided it was no longer worth wasting time in pursuit of the remnants of Hood's forces, Sherman conceived a plan of far greater destructive potential, expressly designed to crush the South's will to fight.

Every building in Atlanta of any military significance would be destroyed. The city reduced to a smoldering ruin, it would then be abandoned, allowing Sherman to lead his army in a march of destruction across Georgia to the coast at Savannah. Sherman left Atlanta on November 15. He reached Savannah on December 21. In his wake, he left a land and a people reduced to prostration. "War is cruelty," he asserted. "There is no use trying to reform it. The crueler it is, the sooner it will be over."

OPPOSITE ABOVE William Tecumseh Sherman.

OPPOSITE BELOW Major General William T. Sherman discusses matters with an artillery officer during the bombardment of Atlanta. Next to Sherman, holding field glasses, is his chief of artillery, Brigadier General William Barry.

ABOVE LEFT These fortifications on the east side of Atlanta show the strength of the city's defenses. Built over the course of a year under orders from Georgia's governor, the 12-mile line encircled the city. Sherman respected the defenses and rather than assault them he chose to cut the railroads into Atlanta.

ABOVE RIGHT William T. Sherman stands at one of the Federal artillery batteries built for the siege of Atlanta. Photographer George Barnard followed Sherman's army group on the campaign and documented key moments and locations.

RIGHT The Battle of Atlanta, July 22, 1864, as portrayed in the Atlanta cyclorama painting. As Sherman attempted to capture the Georgia Railroad into the city on the east side, Hood launched a furious attack against the Army of the Tennessee in the area. Here, a hand-to-hand struggle is fought over the colors of the 15th Illinois.

The Election of 1864

1864

In June 1864, Republicans met in Baltimore, Maryland, to nominate a presidential candidate. Abraham Lincoln won on the first ballot, with former Democrat Andrew Johnson, a Unionist war governor from Tennessee, nominated as his running mate. The combination of Republican/Democrat and Northerner/Southerner made for a true National Union ticket. The term "Republican" was not used in the 1864 campaign; "Union" was emphasized instead. The Democrats, meanwhile, met in Chicago, Illinois, in late August and confirmed the candidacy of former war hero George B. McClellan. Although the convention advanced a peace platform, urging an end to hostilities and eventual restoration of the Union, McClellan ignored it and urged a continuation of the war as the best means of saving the Union.

In the summer of 1864, the war seemed stalemated without signs of victory for either side. In spite of suggestions that Lincoln should suspend presidential elections until the war was over, he felt that it was important to show that the country could not "have free government without elections; and if the rebellion could force us to forgo, or postpone a national election, it might fairly claim to have already conquered and ruined us."

Mr. Lincoln. "Mike, remove the Salmon and bring me a Tod."
Mike. "The Tod's out; but can't I fitch something else, Sir?"

Yet even Lincoln had serious reservations about his chances for reelection. On August 23, he wrote the following note:

This morning, as for some days past, it seems exceedingly probable that this Administration will not be reelected. Then it will be my duty to so cooperate with the President-elect, as to save the Union between the election and the inauguration; as he will have secured his election on such ground that he can not possibly save it afterwards.

Lincoln folded the paper so that no one could read its contents and then had his entire cabinet sign it without knowing what they were signing.

Lincoln's great fear was that a new administration controlled by peace Democrats might agree to a compromise that would permit slavery to continue. Frederick Douglass, the leading black abolitionist newspaper editor, was called to the Executive Mansion to discuss with Lincoln how the Underground Railroad might be revived in order to get as many slaves across military lines to freedom before a new administration took control. Indeed, race had become a contentious issue in the election. Democrats invented the word "miscegenation," meaning the mixing of the races, as a racist scare tactic of what would occur if Lincoln and his emancipation policies were allowed to have a second term.

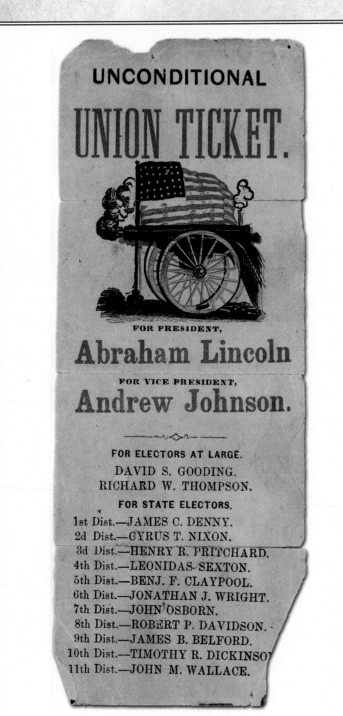

UNCONDITIONAL
UNION TICKET.

FOR PRESIDENT,
Abraham Lincoln
FOR VICE PRESIDENT,
Andrew Johnson.

FOR ELECTORS AT LARGE.
DAVID S. GOODING.
RICHARD W. THOMPSON.
FOR STATE ELECTORS.
1st Dist.—JAMES C. DENNY.
2d Dist.—CYRUS T. NIXON.
3d Dist.—HENRY R. PRITCHARD.
4th Dist.—LEONIDAS SEXTON.
5th Dist.—BENJ. F. CLAYPOOL.
6th Dist.—JONATHAN J. WRIGHT.
7th Dist.—JOHN OSBORN.
8th Dist.—ROBERT P. DAVIDSON.
9th Dist.—JAMES B. BELFORD.
10th Dist.—TIMOTHY R. DICKINSO[N]
11th Dist.—JOHN M. WALLACE.

LINCOLN CLUBS

The 1864 presidential campaign witnessed the absence of the term "Republican Party." Lincoln ran under the National Union banner, and numerous "Lincoln and Johnson Clubs" were formed to raise money for the reelection of the president. Employees at the Executive Mansion formed a club, but with the following caveat: "The within named employees at the Executive Mansion, Contribute sums set against our respective names, as Unconditional Union Men but most respectfully withhold the right of joining any Club, or Political Association whatever."

It is generally conceded that Major General William T. Sherman's capture of Atlanta on September 2 convinced many voters that the end of the war was in sight. Unionists pointed to peace Democrats as being disloyal and defeatist, while Democrats criticized Lincoln as a dictator for his suspension of civil liberties, such as habeas corpus, and the banning of newspapers from printing anything considered disloyal or incendiary. Most Americans, it seemed, came to the conclusion that people don't swap horses in midstream, for Lincoln won with 2.2 million popular votes to McClellan's 1.8 million. The soldiers' vote gave Lincoln a greater margin of 116,887 to McClellan's 33,748. From the soldiers' perspective, the war needed to be fought until the South surrendered unconditionally, and most saw the eradication of slavery as an essential component of a military victory.

OPPOSITE RIGHT A Lincoln-Johnson flag used during the 1864 campaign.

OPPOSITE LEFT In early 1864 Secretary of the Treasury Salmon P. Chase was hoping to get the Republican nomination for president instead of Lincoln. In the end his campaign was unsuccessful and in late June Chase offered to resign from his cabinet post. Although he probably meant this as an empty gesture, Lincoln accepted the resignation and nominated former governor David Tod as a replacement. Tod refused on the grounds of ill health.

RIGHT A cartoon celebrating Lincoln's victory in the 1864 election, suggesting, by having him appear taller, that his reelection has increased his political stature.

LEFT A political ticket promoting Abraham Lincoln and Andrew Johnson. Note the absence of the word "Republican" on this ticket.

The Confederacy Reduced

1861–1865

Jefferson Davis stood in front of the capitol building in Montgomery, Alabama, on February 18, 1861, to become the provisional president of the Confederate States of America. Much of the new Confederate constitution resembled its 1789 counterpart, the Constitution of the United States, save that the president served one six-year term and there was a greater recognition of states' rights as well as the protection and expansion of slavery. It was ratified on November 6, 1861, at the same time as the election of Jefferson Davis. He took the oath of office on February 22, 1862, and the Confederate capital was relocated to Richmond, Virginia.

While advocates from the lower Southern states led the cause for independence, they also had a greater stake in slavery. Almost half of their population was made up of slaves, in contrast to less than one-quarter of the upper Southern states. Similarly, 37 percent of white families in the lower

MAP OF THE **SOUTHERN STATES**, INCLUDING RAIL ROADS, COUNTY TOWNS, STATE CAPITALS, COUNTY ROADS, THE SOUTHERN COAST FROM DELAWARE TO TEXAS, SHOWING THE HARBORS, INLETS, FORTS AND POSITION OF BLOCKADING SHIPS.

PRESENTED To the SUBSCRIBERS of **THE SUN.** January 4th, 1862. MOSES S. BEACH, Proprietor.

Virginia, the South lacked foundries for making heavy cannons and other weapons. Confederate troops suffered from the lack of tents, uniforms, shoes, and blankets. Railroads were underdeveloped in the South, because the region had relied entirely upon the North to supply iron rails and locomotives. The one commodity that was plentiful in the South, of course, was cotton. It was hoped that British and French demand for cotton would eventually bring recognition and support to the Confederacy; crop failures in Europe, however, made them equally dependent upon Northern grain exports. Thus a policy of European neutrality toward the South remained in force throughout the war.

Inflation characterized much of the Southern experience throughout the conflict. Davis was dependent upon state governments to collect tariffs and taxes, and most chose to pay with their own state notes. The Confederate Congress tried to raise funds through the sale of bonds, but found that printing treasury notes was the most expedient way of financing the war. Because of insufficient revenue to support the notes, however, inflation set in, quickly followed by rampant counterfeiting.

A lack of political parties also made legitimate dissent and opposition difficult, and internal dissent arose as non-slaveholders questioned why they were fighting to preserve rich men's property. Suspension of civil liberties in the South was perhaps greater than anything Lincoln had done in the North, undermining the purity of the Southern cause.

As war shortages and inflation became more severe, letters to Confederate soldiers in the field urged them to return home to provide for their families. Desertion rates increased throughout 1864, and in the final months of the war men returned home in record numbers. Many realized that the end of Confederate independence was near.

Southern states owned slaves, compared with only 20 percent in the upper South. Slavery alone, therefore, could not hold the Confederacy together. Moreover, because of racist ideology, much of the South's potential military manpower could be found among slaves, but fear of arming blacks prevented this consideration—until it was too late in the war to make a difference. The issue of states' rights at times confused the issue of national identity, since it made it difficult for Davis and the government in Richmond to compel states to acquiesce to taxation.

A great disparity in industrial and manufacturing output placed the mainly agricultural South at a disadvantage. Except for the Tredegar Iron Works in

OPPOSITE ABOVE The first Confederate cabinet. From left: Secretary of the Navy Stephen Mallory, Attorney General Judah Benjamin, Secretary of War Leroy Pope Walker, President Jefferson Davis, military advisor Robert E. Lee, Postmaster General John Regan, Secretary of the Treasury Christopher Memminger, Vice President Alexander Stephens, and Secretary of State Robert Toombs.

OPPOSITE BELOW A map created in 1862 showing the Confederate States of America.

ABOVE William Seward. He was Secretary of State under Abraham Lincoln and Andrew Johnson from 1861 to 1869.

LEFT The second in a series of five envelopes showing the relationship between Jefferson Davis and Abraham Lincoln as a boxing match. In the series, Lincoln soundly beats Davis.

The Thirteenth Amendment

The Emancipation Proclamation changed the meaning of the Civil War, moving it being beyond a war for Union to one for emancipation and freedom. Lingering doubts about whether the proclamation could withstand legal challenges in the war's aftermath meant that the passage of a constitutional amendment was necessary. Lincoln realized how the proclamation changed the dynamic of the conflict, and believed that whatever questions or deficiencies remained, the passage of the Thirteenth Amendment would be "a King's cure for all the evils."

The president's commitment to ending slavery is readily apparent in his consistent prodding and support for passage of the Thirteenth Amendment. As there had not been an amendment to the Constitution for many decades (the Twelfth Amendment had been passed in 1804), the Constitution had come to take on the aura of a sacred text. Republicans had introduced a resolution late in 1863 to support an amendment to abolish slavery. After

LEFT The passage of the Thirteenth Amendment is shown as breaking the shackles of slavery in the cartoon "Uncle Abe's Valentine Sent by Columbia."

BELOW The House of Representatives erupts in celebration at the enactment of the Thirteenth Amendment in 1865.

THE PRO-SLAVERY THIRTEENTH AMENDMENT

Just prior to the war's outbreak, Thomas Corwin, a Republican representative from Ohio, drafted an amendment in a last-minute attempt to prevent the breakup of the country. In Corwin's Thirteenth Amendment, Congress was prohibited from interfering with "the domestic institutions" of any state, including "persons held to labor or service by the laws of said state." Passed by the House and Senate right before the end of the 36th Congress on March 2, 1861, it was duly sent on to the states for ratification. Only two states, Ohio and Maryland, ratified it, however, and the start of the war that it was supposed to prevent made its adoption moot.

LEFT A print of the final Emancipation Proclamation issued to commemorate it. Sadly, Lincoln did not live to see the Thirteenth Amendment fully ratified.

BELOW A color lithograph of Henry Highland Garnet, an American clergyman and abolitionist. Two weeks following the passage of the Thirteenth Amendment, Garnet delivered a spirited address commemorating the great act. He was the first black to deliver an address in Congress.

reviewing a number of drafts, the Senate Judiciary Committee presented the following to the Senate for their consideration:

Section 1. Neither slavery nor involuntary servitude, except as a punishment for a crime whereof the party shall have been duly convicted, shall exist within the United States, or any place subject to their jurisdiction.

Section 2. Congress shall have the power to enforce this article by appropriate legislation.

All constitutional amendments required a two-thirds approval by congressional vote. The Senate passed it on a vote of 38–6 on April 8, 1864. However, just over two months later on June 15, the House of Representatives rejected the amendment by a vote of 93–65. Democratic opposition defeated the proposal, given that only four House Democrats supported the measure.

Even so, Edwin D. Morgan, chairman of the Republican National Party, added the amendment to the Republican platform at Lincoln's request, an action that further defined the differences between Republicans and Democrats who remained silent in their platform on the slavery issue. Lincoln's reelection allowed him to continue to pressure Congress in his annual message of December 6, 1864:

In a great national crisis, like ours, unanimity of action among those seeking a common end is very desirable—almost indispensable....In this case the common end is the maintenance of the Union; and, among the means to secure that end, such will, through the election, is most clearly declared in favor of such constitutional amendment.

On January 31, 1865, after much discussion and behind-the-scenes dealings, the resolution was eventually passed by the House 119–56, with 13 Democrats having changed their votes. Lincoln signed the document the following day, even though his signature was not actually necessary. Illinois, Lincoln's home state, ratified it on February 1 as a sign of solidarity with the president. Immediately, members of Congress began circulating commemorative editions for their own personal papers. Regrettably, Lincoln did not live to see the amendment ratified by three-quarters of the states; that occurred on December 6, 1865, more than seven months after his death.

The Thirteenth Amendment was the first in a series of other amendments issued by Republicans to protect the rights of newly freed slaves. By embracing constitutional protection, Republicans hoped to redefine the Constitution to reflect the nation's "new birth of freedom" that had been advanced by Lincoln at Gettysburg.

Appomattox: The Final Surrender

Wilmer McLean had brought his family to the gentle rolling pastures of Appomattox County, Virginia, in 1863. A farmer by trade, McLean sought the peace and quiet of farming in one of the few areas of Virginia not torn apart by years of devastating war. McLean had seen enough of the hell of war firsthand; he moved his family from Manassas County, Virginia, where the family farm was overrun and his crops trampled by soldiers in two major battles. In April 1865, Union and rebel soldiers would literally end up at McLean's doorstep, under far different circumstances.

After the fall of Petersburg, which followed the "Waterloo of the Confederacy" at Five Forks, General Robert E. Lee hoped to withdraw his forces to the west on April 3, in order to begin a march south to rendezvous with the force commanded by General Joseph E. Johnston. But his army needed food, and although supplies were reported to be on railcars at Amelia Court House, those cars contained only ammunition. Lee then sent his men into the countryside to forage for food. But they were running out of time. Grant ordered Major General Philip Sheridan's cavalry to pursue the remnants of Lee's army, blocking their intended route and forcing Lee to change his army's course due west to Lynchburg.

On April 5, Lee found Sheridan's cavalry blocking the road to Lynchburg. The rebels turned north, and weary Confederates fell by the wayside, only to be captured by the Federals in close pursuit. The next day, April 6, the Federals attacked Lee's rearguard, which was accompanying the wagon trains along a stream called Sayler's Creek. Although fighting broke out in several sectors, the Federals prevailed, and at Sayler's Creek Lee lost one-quarter of his remaining force in the last major action of the Army of Northern Virginia.

The following day, Grant sent a message to Lee under a flag of truce, proposing surrender terms to the rebels struggling toward Lynchburg. A dialogue started, but Grant was unwilling to accept Lee's proposal for a restoration of peace, and the negotiations broke down. On Palm Sunday morning, April 9, Lee's exhausted soldiers attempted to break through Sheridan's troops, blocking the road at Appomattox Court House. Two corps of infantry supported Sheridan, virtually surrounding the Confederates. Lee rejected the idea that his army take to the hills to fight a guerrilla war. He initiated an exchange of messages with Grant asking for surrender terms.

THE LAST BATTLES

As the Army of Northern Virginia was fighting its last battles, action in other theaters also wound down. Sherman's army group advanced north through the Carolinas and defeated forces assembled by General Johnston at Bentonville, North Carolina, March 19–21. The final resistance at Mobile was broken with Federal victories at Spanish Fort and Fort Blakeley in early April. Scattered fighting continued in the Trans-Mississippi region, with the last battle of the war occurring at Palmito Ranch, Texas, May 12–13, 1865.

ABOVE: The home of Wilmer McLean, Appomattox Court House, Virginia. The end of four long years of war effectively came in the parlor of this house with the surrender of the Army of Northern Virginia.

LEFT A sketch of the Battle of Bentonville, March 19–21, 1865.

OTHER SURRENDERS

After Appomattox other Confederate forces began to lay down arms. Johnston surrendered the second largest rebel army to Sherman in North Carolina on April 26. News of this and Jefferson Davis's flight forced Richard Taylor's surrender in Alabama on May 4. While some Confederates in the Trans-Mississippi fled to Mexico hoping to revive the struggle, Simon Buckner ended official resistance there on May 26 in New Orleans. The last Confederate general to surrender was Cherokee leader Stand Watie, on June 23, 1865.

LEFT Five unnamed Confederates who sought to prolong the conflict after Appomattox.

BELOW This modern painting corrects errors in previous portrayals of the scene inside the McLean parlor on April 9, 1865. Ulysses S. Grant shakes hands with Robert E. Lee as officers of the Army of the Potomac look on and aides attend to the letters detailing terms.

That same afternoon, Lee and Grant met in the parlor of Wilmer McLean's house, just across the square from Appomattox Court House. Grant later recalled his thoughts: "What General Lee's feelings were, I do not know, as he was a man with much dignity with an impassable face, it was impossible to say whether he felt inwardly glad that the end had finally come, or felt sad over the result and was too manly to feel it. But my own feelings, which had been quite jubilant on the receipt of the letter, were sad and depressed. I felt like anything rather than rejoicing at the downfall of the foe which fought so long and valiantly and suffered so much for the cause. The cause was, I believe, one of the worst for which a people ever fought. I do not question, however, the sincerity of the great mass of those who were opposed to us." On April 12, the Federal army marched into the square at Appomattox Court House. Soon, the tattered but proud rebel soldiers filed between solemn lines of Union soldiers, stacked their arms, and furled their flags. The war in Virginia was over. The end of the Confederacy was not far behind.

Lincoln and Reconstruction

1861–1865

A widespread assumption exists that had Lincoln not been killed, Reconstruction with the South would have been dramatically different. Whether or not that is true will never be known. What is known is that Lincoln did not wait for the war to end to begin efforts at reconstructing loyalty to the Union. Rightly or wrongly, the president believed there was widespread Unionist support in most of the South. In his July 4, 1861, message to Congress, he stated: "It may well be questioned whether there is today, a majority of the legally qualified voters of any State, except perhaps South Carolina, in favor of disunion." This view prevented Lincoln from taking measures that might have seemed extreme to Southerners.

When Union victories in 1862 provided Lincoln with portions of Tennessee, North Carolina, Arkansas, and Louisiana, he took immediate steps to place military governors in charge. They were to rally Unionist sentiment and rebuild loyal governments that would undermine Confederate sympathies and place states on the road to being readmitted to the Union. Andrew Johnson had some success in developing a loyal government in Tennessee, and Louisiana elected two members to the House of Representatives, but they were denied seats owing to the continued dispute over whether the president or Congress should control Reconstruction.

On December 8, 1863, Lincoln issued his Proclamation of Amnesty and Reconstruction. Offering amnesty to Southerners who would swear an oath of loyalty to the Union, the president hoped to build a core group of 10 percent of the voting populace that had existed in 1860. Individuals who took the oath also were bound by future acts of Congress and presidential decrees. Any new state constitution had to abolish slavery. Lincoln's plan did not exempt high-ranking Confederate officials.

Radical Republicans in Congress did not think the plan was severe enough and advanced their own on July 2, 1864, known as the Wade-Davis Bill. The bill required half of the prewar voting population to take an oath of allegiance to the U.S. Constitution and obey any laws issued by Congress or the president regarding slavery. Only those who indicated they had never supported the rebellion could be delegates to write a new state constitution, and the new document had to contain a provision abolishing slavery and repudiating the Confederate debt. The bill also barred both Confederate civil servants and

FREEDMEN'S BUREAU

The question of how to help former slaves to adapt to their new status as free people was debated within Congress. Several military officers were already overseeing successful experiments with letting blacks operate former plantations on the South Carolina Sea Islands. Schools were established on the South Carolina Sea Islands as well as other Union-controlled areas in the South to teach former slaves how to read and prepare for postwar life. On March 3, 1865, all of these activities became consolidated into the Bureau for the Relief of Freedmen and Refugees, which became responsible for the care, feeding, and education of four million former slaves.

ABOVE CENTER Abraham Lincoln sat for photographer Anthony Berger on February 9, 1864. Several weeks later, he would be nominated to run for a second term, allowing Lincoln to continue to guide the war and lay a foundation for Reconstruction.

LEFT Former slaves start at the Misses Cookes' School Room at the Freedmen's Bureau in Richmond, Virginia.

military officers from participating in the new governments, and authorized the removal of their citizenship.

Lincoln refused to sign the bill, claiming that he did not wish to be bound by a single plan. Also he did not want to disrupt the governments already installed in Arkansas and Louisiana. Plus, he had doubts about Congress's ability to abolish slavery short of a constitutional amendment. Because Congress had adjourned, Lincoln's refusal to sign it meant the bill never became law.

At the time of his death, many things were still unclear, and these would have influenced what Lincoln did with regard to Reconstruction. As he stated to newspaper editor Albert G. Hodges on April 4, 1864, "I claim not to have controlled events, but confess plainly that events have controlled me." However, Lincoln was not passive in waiting for change, but he knew that his ability to adapt to changing circumstances surrounding Reconstruction required flexibility and sensitivity.

ABOVE A studio portrait of Major General Nathaniel Prentiss Banks. After being removed from field command in 1864, Lincoln put Banks on leave in Washington, and Banks lobbied in favor of Lincoln's plans for the Reconstruction of Louisiana.

RIGHT A painting of Lincoln delivering his final speech on April 13, 1865, to crowds outside the Executive Mansion in which he described his plans for Reconstruction, little knowing that he would not live to see these implemented.

Assassination: Death of the Savior

APRIL 14, 1865

Before Lincoln left Springfield, Illinois, he received numerous death threats and gifts of poisoned food from Southern sympathizers. Although Lincoln and his associates did not believe that assassination attempts were likely, neither did they dismiss credible threats. The president's private secretary, John Nicolay, asserted that all threatening letters sent to the president should be thoroughly investigated. Typically, though, there was not enough information to provide authorities with any insight as to who wrote them or where the letters had come from. Military guards at the Executive Mansion and the Soldiers' Home (which Lincoln used during the summer to escape the disease that ran rampant in Washington) gave the appearance of security, but Lincoln often traveled to and from the War Department and the Soldiers' Home without any escort.

The Civil War divided many families, including the Booths of Maryland. The family represented generations of actors. Edwin Booth was intensely loyal to Lincoln and the Union. While waiting for a train in 1864,

BOOTH AND HIS ASSOCIATES.

LEFT John Wilkes Booth (center) and his coconspirators. Clockwise from top: George Atzerodt, Edmund Spangler, Michael O'Laughlin, Lewis Payne (also known as Lewis Thornton Powell), Samuel Arnold, and David Herald.

BELOW A painting depicting how Booth's assassination of Lincoln in a box at Ford's Theatre might have looked.

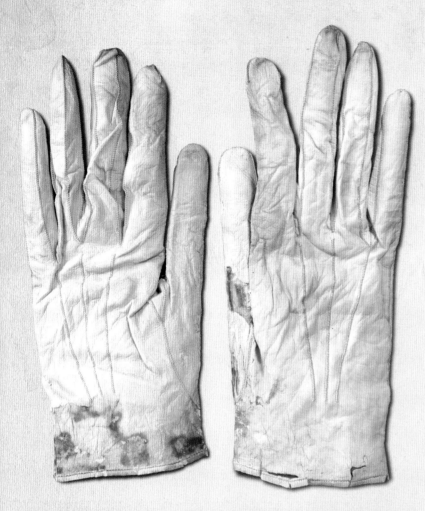

The announcement of Lincoln's attendance at the soldiers' benefit performance of *Our American Cousin* the evening of April 14, 1865, at Ford's Theatre in Washington was widely publicized. Even though it was Good Friday, one of the most sacred days of the Christian calendar, the Lincolns were committed to attending the event. Accompanying them were Major Henry Rathbone and his fiancée, Clara Harris, daughter of New York senator Ira Harris.

Booth's celebrity status was enough to gain him entrance to any theatrical event or access to any individual. Knowing the play, he waited for the largest laugh line before firing his single-shot derringer point-blank at the president's skull. In a brief scuffle with Rathbone, Booth pulled out a knife and stabbed him several times. Freed from Rathbone's grasp, the actor performed a theatrical leap of 10 feet from the president's box onto the stage. He broke his ankle upon landing but stood upright and yelled "Sic semper tyrannis!" ("Thus always to tyrants!") He then hobbled to the exit and the stage door to his horse, which was awaiting him in the alley.

Edwin saw a young man slip on the railroad platform and head for the wheels of a departing train. Reacting instinctively, he reached out and grabbed the man, pulling him back to safety. The young man was Robert Todd Lincoln, eldest son of the president. In contrast, Edwin's youngest brother, John Wilkes Booth, was a loyal supporter of Jefferson Davis and the Confederacy. At his core, John Wilkes Booth was a white supremacist who believed in black inferiority and slavery. A bit of a rake, Booth made his life as dramatic as the characters he played on stage. Throughout the Civil War, his income exceeded $20,000 annually, which allowed him to indulge in a lavish lifestyle.

As Union victory seemed more certain, Booth conspired to kidnap Lincoln en route to the Soldiers' Home late in 1864. The plan was to hold the president in return for the release of Confederate prisoners of war. Booth believed that these soldiers would want to return to battle Union forces. Failing in this attempt, the actor was angered by Lincoln's speech of April 11, 1865, in which he addressed Louisiana's efforts to rejoin the Union. Noting that the new state constitution was a good beginning but not perfect, the president stated: "It is unsatisfactory to some...that the elective franchise is not given to the colored man." Booth turned to his colleague Lewis Powell and declared, "That means nigger citizenship. Now, by God, I will put him through. That will be the last speech he will ever make."

ABOVE Lincoln's gloves were stained with his blood when Booth shot him at Ford's Theatre.

RIGHT A studio portrait of John Wilkes Booth. The spelling mistake in Booth's name was done by the unknown owner of the portrait who struggled with spelling.

BOOTH'S SECRET LOVE

John Wilkes Booth, an actor by trade, is often portrayed as a charming rake with a girl in every town in which he performed. In the late 1980s, however, letters written by Booth to a young Boston socialite, Isabel Sumner, surfaced when Lincoln collector Louise Taper purchased them from a family descendant. Booth seems to have been smitten by her and sent her signed photographs, along with locks of his hair, a ring, a silk scarf, and numerous letters professing his love. The letters continued through late 1864, just months before he would assassinate President Lincoln.

JOHN WILKS BOOTH
THE ASSASSION of
PRESIDENT. A. LINCOLN
J. WILKS. BOOTH

Lincoln's Last Hours and Funeral

Within minutes of Booth's derringer shot, military surgeons reached the presidential box and began to examine Lincoln's wound. Charles Leale, Albert King, and Charles Taft attended to the immediate medical needs. Major Rathbone was bleeding profusely—Booth's stab wounds had severed an artery. Believing Lincoln to have been stabbed as well, Leale and Taft began removing or cutting off the president's collar, shirt, and coat in search of knife wounds. Finding none, Leale ran his fingers through Lincoln's hair and found the bullet wound. The bullet had entered the left side of the president's skull and lodged under his right eye. All agreed that the wound was mortal.

Knowing that Lincoln would not survive a carriage ride back to the Executive Mansion and not wanting the president to die in a theater, the surgeons arranged for a number of soldiers to carry his limp body across the street to a boardinghouse owned by William Petersen. Lincoln's body was placed diagonally atop a bed, his six-foot-four-inch frame being too long to lie horizontally in the bed frame. A death watch began. Secretary of War Edwin Stanton took up a command post in the Petersen house, collecting depositions from eyewitnesses.

There was no doubt that the assassin was John Wilkes Booth. From April 14 to April 26, 1865, Booth was hunted by military forces through Maryland and Virginia. He was finally cornered in a Virginia tobacco barn, refusing to surrender. After setting fire to the barn to force Booth out, a soldier shot and mortally wounded the assassin, and Booth died hours later.

Word came in that an unsuccessful assassination attempt had been made on Secretary of State William Seward. Stanton began to worry that a full-blown conspiracy was underway, and Mary Lincoln became so distraught that Stanton ordered her from the room; eventually she was taken back to the Executive Mansion. Various political and military officials made their way into the Petersen house during the course of the evening. At 7:22 a.m. on Saturday, April 15, 1865, Abraham Lincoln took his last breath. Reverend Gurley offered a prayer. At the conclusion, Stanton uttered, "Now he belongs to the ages."

Lincoln's body was taken to the Executive Mansion, where an autopsy was performed and his remains embalmed. Stanton took over planning for the funeral ceremonies in Washington as well as for the body's rail journey

to Springfield, Illinois. Friends and family attended the ceremony in the Executive Mansion, but Mary Lincoln was still too upset to be present. The body was taken to the Capitol so the public could view Lincoln's remains.

On April 21, Lincoln's casket was placed on a train along with the exhumed casket of his son, Willie. The train stopped at 11 major cities including Baltimore, Harrisburg, Philadelphia, New York City, Albany, Buffalo, Indianapolis, and Chicago, finally arriving in Springfield on May 3. At each stop, the casket was removed and placed on public display. It was estimated that over one million Americans viewed the president's remains, and that another seven million gathered along the rail lines as the funeral train made

its way across America. Ultimately, roughly one in four Americans actively participated in Lincoln's funeral.

In Springfield, approximately 75,000 citizens viewed Lincoln's body in a 38-hour period. The Lincoln home was draped in black bunting, as was the state capitol. Old Bob, the president's horse, was placed in the funeral procession. Also included in the procession were blacks who were joined by Illinois politicians and the governor of Illinois, General Richard Oglesby. As the procession made its way out of town to Oak Ridge Cemetery, Lincoln's casket was put in a temporary receiving vault, with Willie's placed alongside. Both Lincolns had come home for the last time.

OPPOSITE John Badger Batchelder, an engraver, composed this scene placing everyone who was at the Petersen house the morning Lincoln died at his bedside. Realistically, the room was too small to accommodate even a few of those pictured.

ABOVE LEFT Photograph of the Lincoln funeral procession in Washington, D.C.

ABOVE RIGHT A photograph of the receiving vault at Oak Ridge Cemetery in Springfield, Illinois, showing the Lincoln funeral procession, May 4, 1865.

RIGHT The contents of Lincoln's pockets on the night he was assassinated.

LINCOLN'S POSSESSIONS

In 1975, Daniel Boorstin of the Library of Congress stumbled across a wrapped box on a shelf in the library's vault. When he opened it, he discovered that it contained the contents of Abraham Lincoln's wallet and pockets from the night he had been killed. The box had been given to the Library of Congress decades earlier by the president's descendants. The items included two pairs of reading glasses, Confederate currency obtained after the fall of Richmond, nine clipped newspaper editorials, a pocketknife, a handkerchief, a watch fob, and a lens polisher.

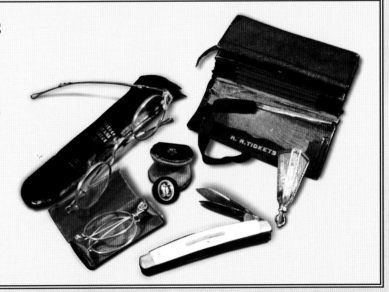

Mary Todd Lincoln: Madness and Sorrow

That Mary Todd Lincoln was a troubled figure at best was clear long before she and her husband arrived in the White House in 1861. She had always been prone to wild mood swings, her "emotional temperament much like an April day," as a cousin wrote of her as a child. As she grew older, so she also developed a thunderous and unpredictable temper. Lincoln's secretaries in the White House never knew whether to expect "Madam" or "the Hellcat." Throughout her life, she suffered debilitating migraines, "the Headache" as these same secretaries ominously knew it. The death of her second son, Eddie, in 1850 at the age of three, sparked an almost complete breakdown.

Lincoln's response to these wild behavioral swings was invariably a phlegmatic, almost indulgent acceptance of them. Of her more extreme outbursts, he remarked: "If you knew how little harm it does me, and how much good it does her, you wouldn't wonder that I am meek."

As First Lady, a title by which she was as much mockingly as respectfully known, she was immediately ill at ease. To sophisticated Washington society, she seemed little better than an "uncouth westerner." The insecurity such snootiness sparked may help explain, if not justify, her reckless, almost willful extravagance as an attempt to impose herself as Mrs. President (or the Republican Queen to her detractors). It is certain that the resulting debts she ran up only added to her persistent neurosis.

She also had to contend with divided loyalties. Many of her numerous siblings were either fighting for the Confederacy or were married to Confederate soldiers. Inevitably, and as a member of a Kentucky slave-owning family, to Northerners she was little better than a rebel herself, and to Southerners a traitor.

Yet however difficult, she was not mad. But bit by bit, a series of events conspired to push her toward the semi-lunacy that clouded her last years. The first was the death of her third son, Willie, in February 1862, an event that left her prostrated with misery and inspired an enduring obsession with spiritualism. (She would claim many times to have been visited by Willie at night, once rushing into her half-sister's room exclaiming: "He lives, Emily!")

ROBERT LINCOLN

For defenders of Mary Lincoln, her son Robert is consistently cast as the villain of the piece. Even if they accept that he was not after her money, as his mother claimed, his action in having her incarcerated is still seen as callous at best. In reality, his concern, first and last, was to protect her. In March 1875 she had suddenly turned up in Chicago convinced he was on the point of death and claiming she was the victim of a poisoning attempt during the journey. She subsequently took to wandering the streets with $56,000 of government bonds sewn into her dress. Lincoln consulted the most eminent experts of the day before having her tried for insanity. One testified she had told him that "an Indian spirit was removing bones from her face and pulling wires out of her eyes." Throughout, Robert proved himself conscientious to a fault. Confronted by his mother's obvious mental disintegration, his patently good intentions cannot be doubted.

OPPOSITE The Lincolns in the White House, depicted in an obviously staged group a matter of months after the death of Willie in February 1862, whose portrait hangs behind them. To the left, Tad and his father; to the right, Mary Lincoln; in the middle, the Lincoln's eldest child, the mustachioed Robert Lincoln, then 20.

LEFT Robert Lincoln, the only one of Abraham and Mary's children to survive into adulthood. He died, rich, distinguished, respected, in 1926 at 82.

BELOW LEFT Elizabeth Keckley was a former slave turned Washington dressmaker who became a close confidante of Mary Lincoln, as well as her dressmaker. Never averse to profiting from the relationship, she was nonetheless a staunch defender of the First Lady.

BELOW If no conventional beauty, Mary Lincoln, seen here in 1861, was a woman who could not merely be formidable but who had a precise sense of her own worth. Yet hers was a life shot through with tragedies that in the end seem to have tipped her into a form of insanity.

It was in one of these "paroxysms of grief" that Lincoln is said to have taken her to a window and, pointing to a lunatic asylum, said, "Mother, do you see that large white building on the hill yonder? Try and control your grief, or it will drive you mad, and we may have to send you there." A less well-documented source has it that Lincoln confided in a colleague that his wife's behavior was "the result of partial insanity."

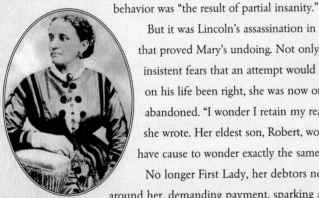

But it was Lincoln's assassination in 1865 that proved Mary's undoing. Not only had her insistent fears that an attempt would be made on his life been right, she was now on her own, abandoned. "I wonder I retain my reason & live," she wrote. Her eldest son, Robert, would later have cause to wonder exactly the same of her.

No longer First Lady, her debtors now crowded around her, demanding payment, sparking an obsessive horror of impending poverty that never subsequently left her. (In fact, her debts settled, she was a rich woman.) The death in 1870 of her youngest son, Tad, necessarily added to her growing derangement.

In 1875, driven to distraction by his mother's bizarre behavior and fearful for her well-being, Robert Lincoln had her sent to a private sanatorium. Under existing Illinois law, the only way he could do this was to have her declared legally insane. She would never forgive him for this "wicked conduct." In the event, she spent only three months there and the following summer she was declared "restored to reason."

Her last years were spent at her sister Elizabeth's house in Springfield, "sitting in the dark with a single candle, packing and unpacking her 64 trunks of clothing." She was 64 when she died on July 16, 1882.

The South: Destitution, Desolation, and Redemption

In 1868, Ulysses S. Grant, the man who more than any other can be said to have secured the Union's defeat of the Confederacy, stood for the presidency of the United States. He did so under a four-word slogan: "Let us have peace." It made plain a disturbing truth. Three years after the end of the war, North and South had still not worked out any practical resolution of their differences. In 1865, in his second inaugural address, Lincoln had spoken of his desire for "a just and lasting peace." Had he lived, he might perhaps have been able to find one. The reality was very different: a simmering hostility between North and South, "a quasi war" as it has been called, that baffled, infuriated and bemused the former and stoked lasting resentment in the latter.

It was resolved, very unhappily, only after the presidential elections of 1876 when the South contrived a rigged political solution that in almost every important respect not merely effectively disenfranchised the nominally free Blacks but confined them to a second-class status that would last almost a century.

In the immediate aftermath of the war, Northern opinion was divided between those who believed the South should be effectively dismembered, the plantation owners disenfranchised, their estates broken up and distributed among freed slaves and, as important, among white Unionists, and those who

THE KU KLUX KLAN

The Ku Klux Klan, founded in Pulaski, Tennessee, in 1865, was just one of a several of white supremacist vigilante groups that were formed in the South, principally the Deep South, in the years after the Civil War. It was largely suppressed in the 1870s, a victim of the Force Acts of 1870–1, which allowed Federal prosecutions of anyone infringing the civil rights of other citizens, in other words the freed slaves, such as preventing them from voting or, as commonly, terrorizing them. The Klan was ostensibly a social club for Confederate veterans, hence the name, said to come from the Greek word *kuklos*, meaning "circle." But it rapidly revealed its true purpose as a terror group, adopting robes, masks, and conical hats both as a disguise and to intimidate. It typically attacked only at night, targeting not just blacks but white Republicans thought to be favorable to blacks. It was paralleled by the White League in Louisiana and the Red Shirts in Mississippi. It resurfaced in the 1920s and remains partly active today.

LEFT Three members of the Ku Klux Klan, captured in September 1871 and shown in the outfits they were wearing at the time of the arrests.

ABOVE The devastation of Broad in Charleston, South Carolina, was repeated across much of the Confederacy, a land left prostrated by the war, its economy as ruined as its infrastructure.

OPPOSITE LEFT The Memphis riots of May 1866 were typical of much of the racial violence that disfigured the Reconstruction. In Memphis, gangs of whites, including policemen, looted the black areas of the city over three days, burning buildings and leaving 48 dead, 46 of them black.

OPPOSITE RIGHT Few issues caused more resentment in the defeated South than the granting of the right to vote to ex-slaves, or freedmen, here seen lining up to vote, a sergeant from the USCT symbolically among them.

believed the most effective way of healing the North–South division was a kind of complete conciliation, every vested Southern interest accommodated, with the obvious exception of slavery.

With more or less calamitous results, Andrew Johnson, vice president to Lincoln and his automatic successor as president after Lincoln's assassination, achieved the unusual feat of embodying both views, his initial hostility to the South transformed into to a desire to conciliate it at almost any price. He succeeded only in provoking bitter resentment on all sides with the consequence that in 1868 he became the first American president to be impeached. He survived by a single Senate vote.

As passions rose on both sides, there was a sense that the nation had almost returned to the divisions of the immediate prewar years, even that the war might almost never have been fought at all. On the one hand, the victors, the Republican North, were attempting to impose a new political settlement— the Reconstruction—designed to reintegrate the shattered South into the Union. And on the other was a growing Southern Democrat resentment at what was seen as a crude attempt to reshape Southern society by providing unreasonable benefits to the freed slaves while simultaneously penalizing white ex-Confederates.

The festering heart of this conflict was of course the fate of the newly freed slaves. The more the North attempted to impose itself on their behalf, the greater the resentment it generated. Increasingly, Southern voices asserted that the South needed to "redeem" itself. It did so by recourse to violence. By the late 1860s, riots, beatings, intimidation, and murder by white supremacists had become commonplace. The foundation of the Ku Klux Klan in Tennessee in 1865 was a precise reflection of Southern resentment of Northern supremacy and an unshakable determination that the second-class status of the Negro should be reinforced.

When Federal troops were sent in to restore order, the result was inevitably more disturbance. By 1875, what became known as the "Mississippi Plan" had been devised. In the name of defending Southern interests, it amounted to little more than a crude attempt to prevent blacks from voting at all. By the 1876 presidential elections, it had been adopted across the South. It resulted in a huge swing to the Democrats. The blacks, free or not, had effectively been disenfranchised. The following year the new Republican president, Rutherford B. Hayes, elected on the slimmest of margins, withdrew all Federal troops from the South.

The Union may have been preserved, but Lincoln's "just and lasting peace" had proved anything but.

Legacy: What It Meant

The assassination of Abraham Lincoln immediately placed him in the pantheon of esteemed American heroes. George Washington may have been the "Father of the Country," but Lincoln now became the "Savior of the Union." The fact that he was shot on Good Friday gave rise to numerous Easter Sunday sermons that compared the Illinois lawyer to the risen Christ. Nor was it lost on other ministers that the president was—in their view inappropriately—at the theater on the highest holy day on the Christian calendar. Despite this, however, to most Americans, Abraham Lincoln had saved the Union and freed the slaves.

Finding concrete expressions of gratitude proved to be more difficult. Efforts by Springfield citizens to build an appropriate tomb that would reflect the greatness of the man were hindered by lack of funding. Private subscriptions were undertaken nationwide in hopes of raising sufficient funds. Black regiments contributed the most to Lincoln's tomb, but it was still not nearly enough for the proposed design drafted by the New England sculptor Larkin Mead. Subsequently, although it was dedicated in 1874, the Lincoln Tomb would not be completed until nine years later in 1883, when its bronze military groupings were put in place.

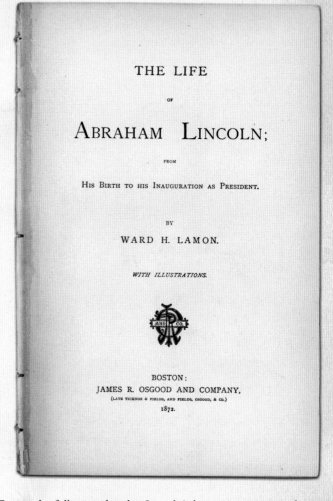

THE LIFE

OF

ABRAHAM LINCOLN;

FROM

HIS BIRTH TO HIS INAUGURATION AS PRESIDENT.

BY

WARD H. LAMON.

WITH ILLUSTRATIONS.

BOSTON:
JAMES R. OSGOOD AND COMPANY,
(LATE TICKNOR & FIELDS, AND FIELDS, OSGOOD, & CO.)
1872.

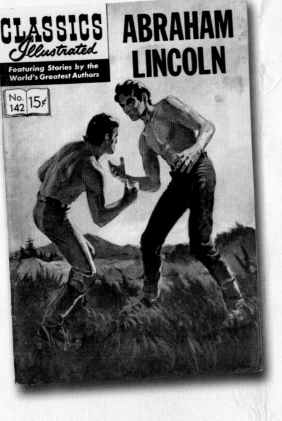

CLASSICS Illustrated
Featuring Stories by the World's Greatest Authors
No. 142 15¢

ABRAHAM LINCOLN

ABOVE RIGHT The first page of Ward Hill Lamon's biography of Lincoln. He was a friend of Lincoln and his bodyguard, although on the night of his assassination Lincoln had sent him to Richmond, Virginia.

RIGHT Long after his death, Lincoln remained a popular cultural figure, appearing in films, on television, in novels, and even in comic books such as the Classics Illustrated comic book series.

During the following decades, Lincoln's legacy was increasingly viewed from the perspective of having preserved the Union, as focus in the country shifted from protecting the interest of freed blacks to promoting reconciliation with white Southerners. Blacks continued to see Lincoln's role as that of emancipator, as witnessed by Frederick Douglass's comments at the dedication of the Freedmen's Monument in Memory of Abraham Lincoln. Claiming that Lincoln "was preeminently the white man's president," and blacks "only his stepchildren," Douglass also recognized the limitations that had guided Lincoln's actions:

Viewed from the genuine abolition ground, Mr. Lincoln seemed tardy, cold, dull, and indifferent; but measuring him by the sentiment of his country, a sentiment he was bound as a statesman to consult, he was swift, zealous, radical, and determined.

In 1908, President Theodore Roosevelt decided to overhaul the designs that were used on American currency, and the first of the new motifs appeared the following year with the Lincoln penny. This coincided with the centennial of Lincoln's birth. The year of 1908 also witnessed a horrible race riot in Lincoln's hometown of Springfield. William Donegan, a black who had made boots for Lincoln, was hanged from a tree. In reaction, the National Association for the Advancement of Colored People (NAACP) was formed in New York on February 12, 1909, in order to combat racial prejudice.

Throughout the twentieth century, Abraham Lincoln's legacy seemed to take on many different shapes and causes. His image was enlisted to sell war bonds in World War I and support New Deal measures during the Great Depression. For an individual who never smoked or drank, his image was used extensively to promote tobacco and alcoholic products such as Old Empire Whiskey; McCormick Distilling Co., which produced a whiskey decanter in the shape of Lincoln; and Old Honest, Los Immortals, Lincoln Bouquet, and La Flor de Lincoln cigars, which used images of Lincoln on their labels. In the twentieth century, cigarette cards were produced featuring scenes from Lincoln's life, including the birthplace cabin and Ford's Theatre. On a more exalted note, Lincoln's powerful writings inspired such figures as Mahatma Gandhi and Dr. Martin Luther King Jr., and the Lincoln Memorial became the appropriate backdrop for the 1963 march on Washington where Dr. King delivered his famous oration, "I Have a Dream."

Another president from Illinois reconnected with the Lincoln legacy. On January 20, 2009, Barack Obama, the first black president of the United States, consciously used Abraham Lincoln to advance an agenda of hope and reconciliation. Taking as his inaugural theme Lincoln's "new birth of freedom," President Obama appealed to Americans' aspirations, just as Lincoln advanced a philosophy of opportunity and human equality.

FLEETWOOD LINDLEY

As a young boy of 13, Fleetwood Lindley thought his father's request to meet him at the Lincoln Tomb was odd. In fact, Lindley was to become one of 23 people who verified the identity of Abraham Lincoln before he was buried a final time in 1901. A grave-robbing attempt in 1876 forced the board of the National Lincoln Monument Association to hide the president's remains within the grounds of the tomb. Examining the remains one final time would end any speculation that Lincoln's body was not in the tomb. Once the casket was sealed, it was placed in a concrete vault with steel bars, and concrete was poured over the casket to prevent any further grave-robbing attempts. Lindley would recount his experience until his death in 1963.

ABOVE Martin Luther King Jr. at the Lincoln Memorial in Washington, D.C.

LEFT Fleetwood Lindley, who witnessed Lincoln's body before it was finally interred in 1901.

Index

Credits

The publishers would like to thank the following sources for their kind permission to reproduce the pictures in this book.

Key. t = top, b = bottom, l = left, r = right & c = centre

AKG Images: 23b
Alamy Images: /Andre Jenny: 17b, /North Wind Picture Archives: 76b, 81r
Alan Scott Walker: 14
Beverly R Robinson Collection, US Naval Academy Museum, MD: 61b
Bridgeman Art Library: 2, 31t, 63l, 63r, /The Huntington Library/Art Collections & Botanical Gardens: 6, /Peter Newark Military Pictures: 61tr, 62t
City of Atlanta: 71b
Cook Collection, Valentine Richmond History Centre: 40b
Corbis: 45b, 75, 80b, 82b, /Bettmann: 51t, 82b, /Medford Historical Society Collection: 81l
Fort McAllister State Historic Site, Georgia Department of National Resources: 47bl
Getty Images: 16b, 20t, 25b, 74t, 77t, 85b, 89r, /Time & Life Pictures: 91t, 91b
Harper's Weekly: 36, 76t
Library of Congress, Prints and Photographs Division: 15t, 15b, 26t, 27b, 33t, 33b, 34-35, 37t, 37b, 38-39, 41b, 47t, 47br, 49br, 52l, 52r, 53b, 56l, 57r, 58b, 58r, 59tl, 59tr, 59b, 60t, 60b, 61tl, 64t, 64b, 65t, 65b, 68t, 69t, 69b, 70t, 71tl, 78t, 78b, 79r, 80t, 82t, 83t, 83b, 87t, 88t, 89l
Lincoln Collection: 8b, 9t, 10-11, 12-13, 16t, 17t, 18-19, 20b, 21t, 21b, 22b, 23t, 24t, 24b, 25t, 27t, 28-29, 30, 31b, 32, 42-43, 44, 45t, 50t, 50b, 51b, 52bl, 52br, 54-55, 62b, 66, 67tl, 66tr, 68b, 72-73, 74b, 75b, 84, 85tl, 85tr, 90r, 90b, 95
Massachusetts Commandery/US Army Military History of the USA, Pennsylvania: 40t, 41t, 46t 46b, 49bl, 56l, Museum of the Confederacy Richmond, Virginia: 49t
National Archives and Records Administration, Washington: 26b, 53tl, 57tr
National Museum of Health and Medicine, Washington DC: 69r
National Park Services: 37tr, 79b
Private Collection: 53tr
Topfoto.co.uk: 67b, /Granger Collection: 8t, 9b, 22t, 48, 71tr, 70b, 77b, 86b, 88b, /The Print Collector /HIP: 87br
US Senate Collection: 57bl
Virginia Tourism: 87bl

MEMORABILIA CREDITS
Abraham Lincoln Presidential Library & Museum: Items 1, 2, 6, 7; American Memory, The Library of Congress: Item 3; National Archives and Records Administration, Washington D.C.: Item 4; Prints and Photographs Division, The Library of Congress: Item 5; Rare Books and Special Collections Division, The Library of Congress: Item 8.

Every effort has been made to acknowledge correctly and contact the source and/or copyright holder of each picture and Carlton Books Limited apologises for any unintentional errors or omissions, which will be corrected in future editions of this book.